D1530219

...BUT I MIGHT NEED IT SOMEDAY!

How to organize your life and WIN the clutter battle once and for all!

Patty Kreamer

Here's to clearing the clutter!

My Best!

Patty Kreamer

ISBN: 0-9720001-1-9 (Paperback)

Library of Congress Control Number: 2002093424

This book is printed on acid free paper.

Printed in the United States of America
Pittsburgh, PA

Dedicated to my husband, George—for helping me "organize" my thoughts and loving me through the process.

…And to the best mom and dad in the world—for giving me the confidence and freedom to be who I am.

TABLE OF CONTENTS

INTRODUCTION 1

CHAPTER ONE:
THE FOUNDATION OF ORGANIZING 3
What Does Being Organized Mean? 3
The Cold Hard Facts 4
How Organizing Is Usually Done 6
Patty's Perspective 8
Your Reasons To Get Organized 13
How To Get The Most From This Book 15

PART I: READY 17

CHAPTER TWO: READY 18
The Circle Of Change .19
A True Story 21
Getting To Know You .24
Why You Are Not Organized 25
Excuses, Excuses! 25
Watch Out For That...Obstacle! 26
You've Got To Listen To Reason! 26
A Closer Look 27
Review 28

CHAPTER THREE: EXCUSES 29
#1 ...But You Might Need It Someday! 30
#2 You Can't Throw Anything Away 32
#3 You Are A True Perfectionist 37
#4 You Are Afraid You'll Fail 40
#5 If You Can't See It, You Forget It! 42
#6 Organizing And Creativity Don't Mix 44

#7 You Don't Think Organizing is Exciting 46
#8 You've Always Done It That Way 48
Review 50

CHAPTER FOUR: OBSTACLES **51**
#1 You Just Have Too Much Stuff! 52
#2 Your Stuff Needs A Home 55
#3 You Have No Time To Clean Up 57
#4 You Have The Wrong Type of Storage 59
#5 You Inherited Systems Or Items 61
#6 You Were Never Taught Organization 63
#7 You Grew Up With Clutter 65
#8 You Find Comfort In Clutter 67
#9 You're A P-R-O-C-R-A-S-T-I-N-A-T-O-R! . . .69
#10 You Don't Set Goals Or Priorities 73
Review 77

CHAPTER FIVE: REASONS **78**
#1 You Have Too Much To Do 79
#2 You Don't Have Enough Space 83
#3 You Remain After A Downsizing 86
#4 You Deal With Difficult People 87
#5 You Are Very Sentimental 89
#6 You Experience A Life–Changing Event 92
Review 96

CHAPTER SIX:
READY TO WRAP IT UP **97**
WHEW! What Does It All Mean? 98
Now What? 99
Review 103

PART II: SET **105**

CHAPTER SEVEN: SET **106**
Look Around At Your Space 107
Ready To Get Set 108
A Decided Activity For The Room 110
A Lot O'Logic 111
A Drawing 114
Exercise 123
Review 125

PART III: GO! **127**

CHAPTER EIGHT: GO! **128**
Two Things Before We Go! 128
Here We Go! 130
Review 136

CHAPTER NINE: "STUFF" CLUTTER . . .**137**
The "Stuff" Clutter System 137
Step 1. Go Through and Sort 137
Step 2. Go Out And Deliver 143
Step 3. Go Home Where You Belong 144
Step 4. Go Into The Right Container 145
Review 146

CHAPTER TEN: PAPER CLUTTER **147**
On To Paper Clutter Systems 147
I've Sorted–Now What? 151
1. Schedule Them 152
2. Use A PaperConnect™ Tickler File 142
The Last Pile–The File Pile! 155
Filing Systems 157

PART IV: MAINTENANCE **169**

CHAPTER ELEVEN:
"STUFF" MAINTENANCE **170**
    Keeping The "Stuff" Away 171
    Need Vs. Want 171
    The Enemy 173
    One In – One Out 175
    One Out – One In 176
    Review 178

CHAPTER TWELVE:
PAPER MAINTENANCE **179**
    Paper Clutter - Stop The Madness! 179
    Incoming! 179
    The Mail 180
    Other Incoming Papers 182
    Bonus Maintenance Ideas 185
    Index It! 185
    Working Backwards 189
    Keeping Tabs 190
    Making A File – What A Drag! 193
    General Maintenance Ideas 195
    Review 197

CHAPTER THIRTEEN: **198**
    Ready, Set, Go! 199
    Real Life Stories 202
    You Are Ready & Set...Now Go! 207
    Appendix 209
    RESOURCES 209
    Quick Order Form 213

What some people are saying about this book:

"Patty Kreamer takes very simple but powerful principles that the reader can easily apply. It's a must read for anyone who is sick of clutter and chaos. Her step-by-step guide is guaranteed to lead the way to a more productive and satisfying life."

—Eleanor Schano, Broadcast Journalist, TV Host "Agewise", WQED Pittsburgh

"At last, painless surgery that cuts through to the real cause of clutter rather than treating surface symptoms. But I Might Need It Someday is not a quick-fix pill. It is a life-changing system that will keep you and your environment in tip-top shape. Read it in good health."

—Harold Taylor, author of *Making Time Work For You*

"Patty Kreamer dives deep and gives an in-depth, thought-provoking account of the beliefs that cause so many to feel as if they're drowning in a sea of clutter. Patty generously shares the wisdom needed to get back above water once more. 'But I Might Need it Someday' is an excellent read for anyone who is serious about taking the journey to a clutter-free, organized life."

—Maria Gracia, *www.getorganized.com*

"*Patty has done a great job in breaking down a subject that can be overwhelming into components that are manageable and realistic. I have used the techniques she describes and can now find things that have been missing mysteriously for years!*"

—Susan Owens, Owner, Word Systems Associates

"*'...But I Might Need it Someday!' is a must for anyone that has struggled with "stuff" or paper clutter...this book has put me on a clutter diet!*"

—Terri Sokoloff, CBI, CRB, GRI, Broker, President Specialty Bar & Restaurant Brokers

"*If you really want to organize and simplify your life, get your copy of 'But I Might Need It Someday.' Patty Kreamer makes it as easy as READY, SET, GO! Now you'll find what you need when you need it.*"

—Jim Donovan, author, *Reclaim Your Life*

ACKNOWLEDGEMENTS

A sincere thanks to:

Michelle Belan—for all of your hard work in editing this book over and over until you knew it would make us proud, and not a moment sooner.

Mark Murdzak—for putting life into the cover and illustrations. murdzak@yahoo.com

Susan Owens—for taking such an interest in the success of this book and contributing to its final overall shape that it turned into.

Shirley Englert (a.k.a. Mom), Kathy Brown, Eleanor Schano, Lillian Vernon, Stephanie Denton, Harold Taylor, Maria Gracia, Anita Brattina, Leslie McKee, Jim Donavan, and Terri Sokoloff—for taking precious time to read this book and offer valuable feedback.

JoAnn McBride and Kevin Lamb—for your contribution to the last chapter. Your input is so appreciated.

Cornelia Karaffa—for the photographs in the book. Your eye is the best I've ever seen!

Dennis Snedden—for your valued wisdom.

Jeff Tobe, Joanne Sujansky, and Jim and Ann Marie Kwaiser—for inspiring me as my mentors!

And to Ted Novak…just because.

MY INTENTIONS WITH THIS BOOK ARE:

1. To help you discover what keeps you from being organized.
2. To provide you with the necessary tools to declutter and simplify your life.
3. To help you design and implement strategies to overcome your excuses, obstacles, and reasons for disorganization.
4. To help you create systems and maintain your newly-organized environment.
5. To coach you when the excuses, obstacles, and reasons threaten to return.
6. To help you determine when to call a professional organizer for help.

This book contains sample scenarios, applications, and systems that are available as tools to help you reach your organizing goals, whatever they may be.

So put your organizing engine in gear and prepare to learn simple solutions to those problems that have been plaguing you for as long as you can remember.

Here's to simplifying your life!

Patty Kreamer

INTRODUCTION

Congratulations! You have just made the best choice in books if you are ready to organize your life and WIN the clutter battle once and for all! So put on your seatbelt and hold tight—you're in for a fun ride!

You may have read many books about how to get organized and here you are, about to read yet another. Or perhaps this is your first book on organizing. Whatever the case, if I have my way, it will be the last book on organizing you'll ever need to read.

"Out of clutter, find Simplicity.
From discord, find Harmony.
In the middle of difficulty lies opportunity."

Albert Einstein, Scientist

CHAPTER ONE:

The Foundation of Organizing

WHAT DOES BEING ORGANIZED MEAN?

I have good news for you—being organized does NOT have to mean being neat! Isn't that a relief? What being organized DOES mean is being able to find things when you need them...not 3 weeks later. Let's look at two situations.

1. Julie is in her office and she receives a phone call from her boss. He tells her he is stopping by her office in 10 minutes. What is the first thing that Julie does? She starts shoving all the clutter into drawers, boxes, and cabinets. When her boss arrives, he sees nothing but a neat environment. Does this mean that Julie is organized? No!

2. On the other hand, Bob has piles of clean laundry in his bedroom...some on the dresser, some on the bed, a bit on the nightstands, and even some on the floor. It is not a pretty sight, but Bob knows exactly where to find his socks, pants, shirts, and underwear. Is Bob organized? Yes!

You don't have to live in a sterile, boring environment to be organized. You just have to have effective systems that work for you.

THE COLD HARD FACTS

Being disorganized doesn't mean you are a bad person, and isn't necessarily a reflection on a person's character at all. In most cases, a person is disorganized not because of some character flaw, but because his system of managing paper and "stuff" needs a tune-up. And sometimes, there is no system at all. Having said that, however, being disorganized does tend to reflect poorly on a person, and unfortunately, people may judge you if your home or office is in chaos. You may come across as incompetent because you can't find an important file. Just as importantly, there are financial costs to being disorganized as well. If you don't think that being disorganized is a big deal, let me demonstrate in a measurable way that it is, especially in the work place.

Being disorganized means constantly having to search for things. If you spend just five minutes of each hour of an 8-hour day looking for things, that adds up to over four wasted weeks a year!

HERE'S HOW:

5 min./hour X 8 hours/day = 40 min./day

40 min./day = 200 min./week

200 min./week = 10,000 min./year

10,000 min./year = 166 hours

166 hours = 20.75days

20.75 days = 4.15weeks/year

Thus, if you are paying a person $10/hour, faulty systems and disorganization are costing you $10/hour X 166 hours OR **$1660/year!** And that's just one person! If you multiply that times the number of disorganized people in your company, it can be staggering.

Now, if *you* are disorganized, figure what your time is worth and multiply it by 166 hours. Do you like what you see? I didn't think so.

The worst part is (yes, it gets worse!) that most people spend MORE than five minutes of every hour trying to find misplaced items. The reality is that most people waste an average of SIX weeks per year! The calculations above use conservative estimates, but they make the point. So the next time you spend five minutes looking for something, ask yourself if it's worth it to get organized. I think you'll agree that it is.

HOW ORGANIZING IS USUALLY DONE

Let's say you have a mess in your office. You get in that mood to straighten up, which usually means you are so disgusted with how your office looks that you can't take it any more. So you run around throwing things into drawers, closets, boxes, or crevices—any space that is hidden.

You step back a few hours later and admire your work. It is a masterpiece! The room looks so neat that you can't believe your eyes—that is, as long as you don't open the closet doors, look under the bed, behind the desk, or on the other side of the file cabinet. You even leave the room just so you can walk back in and get that rush over and over again. You've never been more proud of yourself!

Then it happens. Within a week, the room is back to the way it was before you got that burst of energy to clean it up. It looks like a tornado has struck. It may even look worse than when you started to clean it up the first time!

The reason this happens is simple: you never took the time to establish SYSTEMS that are designed around the way that you work. You simply put things in a place that was convenient at the moment. To become truly organized, you must pay attention to your habits—those that work and those that don't.

Let's take a look at organizing from a professional's point of view...

PATTY'S PERSPECTIVE

As a professional organizer, my goal is to develop systems for my client that will help him stay organized day in and day out.

To prevent my client from staying mired in the disorganization cycle, I would lead him through a three-step process that is the basis for this whole book. When my client follows this three-step process, the result is a successful, effective, and long-lasting organizing session. Skipping any one step can be detrimental to the results.

Step 1... get <u>READY</u>

Let's use David as an example. First, I spend about an hour with David at his location to explore how we could better organize his environment. I ask several questions to get to know him...how he thinks, how his daily life flows, what his day is "normally" like. About 45 minutes into the hour, a clearer picture emerges based on these questions, and I can identify David's most obvious trouble spots. The piles of papers have grown so big that he can no longer see over them, his telephone is too far from his chair, and his database is out of date. The questions I ask vary from client to client, depending on each client's personality, the severity of the problem, the client's willingness to open up, etc. But for now, I will tailor my questions to get to know David on many levels so that I can design solutions specifically for him. For example, how much of the piled paper on your desk is current? With which ear do you talk on the phone? How often do you access your database?

"If you don't have a vision, then you will always be determined by others' perceptions."

Melanée Addison, Author

9

Step 2...get SET

From Step 1, I know more about David and his personality, what is hindering him, and what systems may be the best for him. Now I need to know:

☆ David's organizing goals.
☆ How David envisions the end result.
☆ If getting organized is a priority for David.
☆ If David has time to invest in getting organized at this time.

This information will allow us to establish David's goals and create a plan accordingly. If we don't know where or how far David wants to go with the organizing and how he is going to get there, we cannot measure our success.

During our meeting we determined that David's goals are: to clear off his desktop, to make using the phone more comfortable, and to clean up his database. In order to do this, we will: design a filing system for the papers on his desk, move the phone to a more logical location, and schedule time to enter his contacts into his database. Goals and plans are key components to accomplishing any challenge, and organizing is no exception.

In this step, we are also determining how David thinks. Does he like to see everything out on his desk or does he work better when there is NOTHING on his desk? We are looking at David's style and thought process. Would colored folders be appealing to David? Or are plain manila and green hanging folders acceptable? Does David think alphabetically, numerically, in categories, or in geographic regions? I listen to David as we discuss his daily routine and from his answers, I can surmise his style and preferences. This is all part of the plan to customize systems for David.

Step 3...<u>GO</u>!

Finally, David and I set up a time for my return to put the plan into action. At that time, we sort through all of the clutter that is plaguing David, making decisions as quickly as possible. Before you know it, the systems that we had planned are quickly taking form. It's a beautiful thing!

The GO part of the process can last anywhere from 2 hours to 252 hours, depending on the nature and volume of the problem and the client's speed for decision-making. I must warn you: it will get ugly before it gets pretty.

By using the READY, SET, GO! System, you too can become organized.

So the next time you go into a room and find that you are overwhelmed by the clutter, try something new. Instead of unconsciously throwing things into any available container, STOP and think about what you are doing. Make an effort to first understand your habits and the logic (or lack of logic) behind them. Only then will you truly be able to conquer your clutter.

YOUR REASONS TO GET ORGANIZED

Before you begin the process of becoming organized, I want you to take a few minutes and think about **why** you want to be organized. What is motivating you to want to be organized? Knowing this answer will keep you focused on your goal, especially when you get discouraged. On the next page is a checklist of some common reasons I have heard over the years. Perhaps some of these will apply to your situation, and if you have other reasons, please add them in the space provided. You may be tempted to skip this exercise, but don't—when you start to feel your enthusiasm for organizing waning, refer back to your answers and focus on the end result.

I WANT:

☐ To spend more time with my family
☐ To get promoted
☐ To set a good example for my children
☐ To set a good example for my staff
☐ To go home on time
☐ To be less stressed
☐ To feel less confused all the time
☐ To be able to have visitors
☐ To have more time for me
☐ To find things when I need them
☐ To be on time instead of being late
☐ To do what I want to do
☐ To have the freedom organization offers
☐ To feel in control of my life
☐ To have people trust me with their stuff
☐ To feel rested...not tired anymore
☐ To live in an uncluttered environment.
☐ _____
☐ _____
☐ _____

HOW TO GET THE MOST FROM THIS BOOK

The READY, SET, GO! System is simple, practical, and easy to remember. This system will be fully explained in the first three parts of the book. I HIGHLY RECOMMEND THAT YOU DO NOT SKIP ANY ONE OF THESE PARTS. If you do, organizational bliss is less likely to take hold. These pages will give you the meat and potatoes (or tofu & sprouts for vegetarian readers) that you have been yearning for—steps that you need to take before, during, and after you organize your life.

PART IV is jammed full with helpful ideas on how to maintain your newly found organization. So turn the page and let's get started!

REVIEW

What does being organized mean?
The cold hard facts
How organizing is usually done
How a Professional Organizer works
   1. Ready...
   2. Set...
   3. Go!
List your reasons to get organized:

_____
_____
_____
_____
_____
_____
_____

How to get the most from this book

NOTES

_____
_____
_____
_____
_____
_____
_____
_____
_____
_____
_____
_____

PART I: READY

> *"Within you right now is the power to do things you never dreamed possible. This power becomes available to you just as you can change your beliefs."*

Maxwell Maltz, Author

CHAPTER TWO:

Ready...

As you get READY, it is a good time to talk about CHANGE. If you just rolled your eyes, there is good news and bad news. The bad news is that if you want to go from being disorganized to being organized, you will have to make *some* changes. The good news is that I believe that it is important to design systems around your current habits so that *as little change as possible* is necessary. For example, if you always walk into the house and throw your keys on the table by the door, I doubt that I am going to persuade you to hang them on a hook. Solution? Put a key tray on the table to catch the keys so they don't go on the floor or hide underneath the mail. No fundamental change is necessary. You just added a tray and your habit stays the same. Keep in mind, however, that sometimes more substantial change is inevitable if you want to achieve your goals.

The Circle of Change below shows the three components needed in order for any change to take place in your life: belief, behavior, and tools. Without any one of these elements, lasting change is improbable.

For now, we are going to delve into **beliefs** and **behaviors**. **Tools** will be added in Part 2 and beyond.

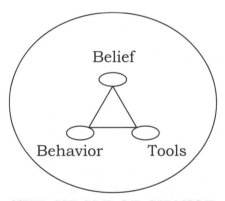

THE CIRCLE OF CHANGE

According to The American Heritage Dictionary, Second College Edition, 1982:

A BELIEF *is a mental acceptance of or conviction in the truth or actuality of something.*

Beliefs include your attitudes, values, and viewpoints. Most beliefs are learned from family and friends over the years, which means that they are able to be changed by accepting new beliefs and letting go of the old.

BEHAVIOR *is the action or reaction of persons or things under specified circumstances.*

What you do in certain situations defines your behavior. Again, this can be changed. Most behavior is ruled by your beliefs, so it is critical that you first analyze and change your beliefs in order to alter your behavior.

For instance, if Shirley believes that she would be happier without the clutter, then she is on the road to being able to change her behavior. However, if she believes that she must keep every item that enters her life, Shirley's behavior will reflect her beliefs and she will continue to keep everything. Change will not occur, and she will still be living with clutter.

If you are unhappy with what your beliefs bring into your life, only you can change them. This may not be easy, but it is possible. Sometimes all that it takes is a little time and common sense to analyze why you believe something. Here is a personal example that may seem silly (because it is), but it gets the point across.

A TRUE STORY

When I was a little girl, I spent a lot of time with my dad. On the night before garbage day, my dad would always collect the garbage in all of the rooms of the house. In the kitchen, the main place for trash, he would only use one garbage bag each week (and this still holds true to this day). It didn't matter if the bag was bursting at the seams (which it usually was). Dad would not pull out another garbage bag. You would have thought that there was a prize each week for the house that had the most garbage in one bag.

Now on the surface, I thought that there must have been a blue law on the books stating that any more than one bag on the curb was illegal (even though I could see more than one bag on the neighbor's curb).

Underneath my dad's behavior was his belief that he should conserve garbage bags because they were expensive. Dad grew up during the Depression; therefore, conserving resources was ingrained in his beliefs.

Years later, I got married and went out on my own. Because I had watched my father collect the garbage for many years, I felt qualified for the job. So I elbowed my husband George away from MY trash as I collected it.

At first, I thought he was envious of how I could expertly fit ten pounds of trash into a bag with only a five-pound capacity. Then I realized that he didn't understand the 1-bag rule. I questioned him with a look in my eyes that oozed pity. I felt sorry for him because he hadn't read THE RULEBOOK when he was growing up.

Unbeknownst to me, he was feeling pity for me because I HAD read THE RULEBOOK as a kid.

Occasionally, it was difficult to fit a whole week's worth of trash into one bag, but I wouldn't give in. George, however, would. He would force me to pull a second bag out for the overflow (and on really big occasions, a third). I didn't die, but it sure didn't feel good.

After a while I questioned myself to see why I felt this need to conserve bags. I realized that it was because of this silly belief that had been instilled in me as a child.

I had to literally ask myself, "Why do I do this?" Then I had to force myself to answer. The answer was that I didn't know any better and it just seemed right.

You will be happy to know that I still collect the trash for garbage day and I have no problem taking out a new bag or two, even on the night of collection! We still laugh about it, but I think I have moved on! (Secretly though, I do try to get by with as few bags as possible!)

So ask yourself, "What do I do that I have NEVER questioned?" Some of the actions that you take may be the result of what you have been taught. You must learn to question the premise of your beliefs to avoid perpetuating ineffective or destructive actions.

GETTING TO KNOW YOU

By examining your beliefs and behavior, you are getting to know YOU better. You now have a pretty good idea as to WHY you want to be organized. The next logical step is to look at why you are NOT. Let's explore some aspects of your life that may be preventing you from getting organized.

WHY YOU ARE <u>NOT</u> ORGANIZED

Three words: EXCUSES, OBSTACLES, and REASONS. These can be your biggest adversaries when it comes to getting organized. They are defined as follows according to The American Heritage Dictionary, Second College Edition, 1982:

<u>EXCUSES, EXCUSES!</u>

EXCUSE: An explanation offered to justify or elicit forgiveness.

An excuse can be corrected by changing your attitude or **beliefs.** If you look at my experience with the trash bags, you'll notice that the only explanation I could give was that my **beliefs** justified my actions. My **behavior** was directly related to my beliefs. Therefore, changing my beliefs was enough to change my behavior.

WATCH OUT FOR THAT...OBSTACLE!

OBSTACLE: One that opposes, stands in the way of, or holds up progress.

An obstacle can be corrected by changing your behavior. Look at Lindsay the shopaholic. She has a habit of buying whatever she wants whenever she wants it. This is a **behavior** that Lindsay needs to correct, because she has too much clutter and feels that she spends too much money. Lindsay can overcome this obstacle by changing her behavior and curtailing her shopping habits.

YOU'VE GOT TO LISTEN TO REASON!

REASON: A declaration made to explain or justify an action, decision, or conviction.

A reason is possibly correctible, but it may be out of your control to do so. There are things in your life that are just not within your control. For example, if you work in a cubicle, your workspace is limited and this may inhibit your ability to stay organized.

A CLOSER LOOK

Let's look more closely at the many EXCUSES, OBSTACLES, and REASONS that hinder the disorganized. As you may have noticed, the biggest difference between these three categories is how you **overcome** them.

If you identify with any excuse, obstacle, or reason listed in the next three chapters, put a check mark in the box beside it. This will help you to identify the challenges to your belief systems and behaviors that need to be assessed in order to make changes.

REVIEW

THE CIRCLE OF CHANGE—Belief, Behavior, and Tools

A BELIEF is a mental acceptance of or conviction in the truth or actuality of something.

BEHAVIOR is the action or reaction of persons or things under specified circumstances.

A True Story
Getting to know you
Why you are not organized
Excuses! *An explanation offered to justify or elicit forgiveness.*
Obstacle! *One that opposes, stands in the way of, or holds up progress.*
Reason! *A declaration made to explain or justify an action, decision, or conviction.*
A closer look

_____

_____

_____

_____

_____

_____

_____

_____

_____

*"The most drastic and usually the most
effective remedy for fear is direct action."*

William Burnham

CHAPTER THREE:

Excuses

... An excuse can be corrected by changing
your attitude or **beliefs.**

1. ...But you might need it someday!
2. You can't throw anything away.
3. You are a true perfectionist.
4. You are afraid you'll fail.
5. If you can't see it, you forget it.
6. Organizing and creativity don't mix.
7. You don't think organizing is exciting.
8. You've always done it that way.

The #1 excuse that I hear...

1. ...BUT YOU MIGHT NEED IT SOMEDAY!

If this is why you keep so much stuff, it may make you feel better to know that you share that belief with many other people. Every client that I work with says this *at least* five times in each organizing session. If your goal is to get organized, the excuse "...but I might need it someday!" is going to hinder your success.

*"You don't always get what you ask for, but you never get what you don't ask for......
unless it's contagious."*

—Franklyn Broude

 Belief Tune-Up

If you keep something because you believe that you MIGHT need it someday, then ask yourself: "if 'someday' arrives and it's not there, what will I do?" The answer usually is "I'll go get another one" OR "I'll make do without it." Many of the items that you keep you don't even know that you have. If you do know that you have them, you likely won't know where they are among the clutter when you need them! Why bother keeping an item for someday if, when "someday" gets here, you'll end up having to get a new one anyway? "But I might need it someday" is a common yet flimsy excuse for hanging on to things. Keeping too much stuff causes you unnecessary stress every time you look at the clutter while wishing it wasn't there. And the real kicker is that when you go to use something that you've been saving, it's probably too tattered to use and you will want a NEW one anyhow.

This excuse blends in with the next one (#2) when it comes to deciding to let go.

☐ 2. YOU CAN'T THROW ANYTHING AWAY.

This is in the same family as #1. Regardless of whether you think you might need it someday or not, you just find it difficult to let go of your belongings. Perhaps you feel guilty because somebody gave you a particular item and you think they will be insulted if they find out you no longer have it. Or perhaps you paid good money for the item and you hate to be wasteful. This guilt is understandable, but it is costing you your peace of mind and happiness. You need to go beyond the guilt and look at what keeping the clutter is doing to you both physically and mentally.

Don't let your clutter control you...
you must control your clutter.

Belief Tune-Up

If you have items that you don't need or want but you find it difficult to throw them away, ask yourself the following questions in reference to your beliefs. Don't just answer the questions; question the answers.

A. Have I used this item in the last _____ days/months/years? Depending on what "it" is, you have to decide what time frame is reasonable.

EXAMPLES:

Clothes—2 seasons without wearing them

Shoes—1 year, if out of style or worn

Books—Outdated or no longer useful (i.e. school or college texts, old software manuals.)

Magazines, newspapers, journals, etc.—If you have subscriptions, the frequency of delivery should govern this. If it's a monthly publication, toss the issue when it's a month old. Toss your daily newspaper when it's a day old. (After all, it's not "news" when it's old!)

Papers—If you are keeping papers because you believe the IRS would prefer that you keep them, speak to your accountant or lawyer about how long you truly need to retain them. If you are keeping utility bills and you never refer to them and you don't use them as a write-off, why are you keeping them? The utility company keeps a record of your bills. A year's worth is the most I recommend keeping. When the current bill comes in, put it in the front of the folder, pull out the oldest from the back and destroy it. (I keep last month's bill until the new bill arrives confirming that they received my last payment). This, of course, assumes that you already have a filing system. If you do not, you will be able to create one after reading this book!

B. Does it still have a use to you?

For example, the bike with the torn banana seat, missing a pedal, draped in spider webs and other unusual creatures—do you see yourself ever using it again?

C. Is it broken or obsolete?

And you are keeping that broken 8-track stereo and beta VCR because...?

D. Can it be fixed?

Many times the item is so old that parts are no longer available because the manufacturer is out of business. I think they are trying to tell you something...time to pitch it.

E. Is it worth fixing?

Even if you fix that old lamp, do you really want it in your home?

F. Can someone else benefit from it more?

If you don't use something, think of all the people that can. It's a win-win situation. You lose the clutter and someone else now has a winter coat.

G. What would happen if I no longer had this in my life?

I sometimes ask my clients, "Imagine coming home one day to find that all the clutter is gone. How would you feel?" They usually reply with a big sigh of relief, followed by "Awesome!" If this is your response, it's time to make some decisions and declutter your life. Get rid of the clutter one decision at a time.

H. If I keep this item because it is attached to memories, are they good memories?

If yes, be sure that you are keeping it for the right reasons and storing it properly. Keeping heirlooms boxed up in trunks in the attic is a sad way to treat treasured memories. If you feel you have no way of properly displaying your mementos, you may want to consider giving them to a family member, selling them, buying a curio cabinet, or designating an area that can be used as a family shrine or museum area.

If your stuff is attached to negative memories, it is probably better to sell it, donate it, give it to a loved one who would appreciate it more, or simply discard it. Why torture yourself?

I. Would I rather have the clutter and the stress that goes with it OR the peace that comes when the clutter goes?

All of these questions make you take a peek at your beliefs and evaluate what you value more. Answering these questions can be difficult as you begin to organize and declutter, but as you see your life becoming more simplified and less stressed, they become easier and easier to answer.

☐ **3. YOU ARE A TRUE PERFECTIONIST.**

Perfectionism is very exhausting. I know—I am a recovering perfectionist. When I was younger, everything had to be just perfect or it couldn't be associated with me. In fact, (I know I'm going to regret writing this) they used to call me Patty Perfect in high school. If it wasn't done 100%, it wasn't good enough!

Sound familiar? If so, let me tell you, the other side is so much easier. I never realized how exhausting it was always trying to be perfect. I would work on something incessantly and it might bring personal satisfaction, but did little to enhance the value of the project. You can do a job at an acceptable level in a fraction of the time it takes to do it perfectly. In reality, is perfection even attainable?

Belief Tune-Up

My friend Susan identifies with perfectionism as one of her main barriers to being clutter-free. Susan grew up in a household with perfectionist parents and a total lack of organization. Susan's dad built their home nearly single-handedly, but he never got around to the finishing touches like paint, wallpaper, or tiles in the ceiling! However, when he built a storage closet, he redid the ceiling twice because it was one-quarter inch out of alignment. Susan's mom made the perfect bed, ironed the perfect shirt, and cleaned a room to within an inch of its life. Because each of these things had to be done perfectly, which was overwhelming, she rarely did them. This resulted in a household that functioned in a perpetual state of clutter. Susan took both the perfectionism and the clutter with her into her adult life. *Once she recognized and freed herself of the perfectionism, she was able to effectively deal with the clutter.*

Many times the reason a perfectionist is disorganized is that she believes that she can't get her room or office to look 100% perfect, so why try? But wouldn't it be better to have an 80% organized office than a 100% cluttered office?

If you find yourself in these shoes, let go of your perfectionist beliefs for a week and see if your life comes crumbling down around your ears. (HINT: It won't). You can do this by letting things lie where they are without constantly straightening them; returning a library book after its due date; handing in a report after your *first* draft; organizing a room for only one hour and being happy with the results. As a recovering perfectionist, I find it liberating to not always strive to be perfect.

Actually, it's not that difficult to be imperfect. Give it a try...you'll be amazed at how much energy you will have for things that you didn't before.

☐ 4. YOU ARE AFRAID YOU'LL FAIL.

Zig Ziglar said, "Failure is never ever a person, it is merely an event on the way to success." If you have tried to get organized without success, it is not necessarily YOU that has failed; it is more likely the systems that you have tried that have failed. If you believe that you won't succeed at organizing, you probably won't even try.

"Failure is the condiment that gives success its flavor."

- Truman Capote, Author

Belief Tune-Up

Successful organization should be driven by and designed around YOUR thought processes, beliefs and habits, not someone else's. Watch how your papers flow. Take note of your lifestyle—examine what works for you and what does not.

Don't look at a bad organizing session as a failure but as an outcome. Outcomes are positive experiences that improve your personal development. If you believe that you are a failure just because something didn't work out exactly the way that you planned it, reevaluate your definition of failure. Colonel Sanders tried to sell his chicken recipe countless times (over 1000!) before someone took him seriously. Many inventors come up against the same walls, but they keep trying and learning from each outcome. Each attempt at getting organized produces better and better results because you have learned from each previous outcome.

5. IF YOU CAN'T SEE IT, YOU FORGET IT!

This is the black hole theory—if you put it away, you might forget you have it because it will get sucked into the "black hole," never to be seen again. But this fear only becomes reality if you don't create a system to prevent it. For instance, if Lauren puts papers in a place where she can't see them, she is afraid she will forget to act on them. With possessions or purchases, the same thing may happen. When Lauren comes home from the store, she sets her purchases on the dining room table so she can remember 1) that she has them and 2) that she needs to do something with them later on. Lauren is afraid that if she puts them away, she'll forget she bought them. But having a hundred new purchases on the dining room table can make it hard to eat dinner comfortably, and difficult to locate the new item when it comes time to use it.

This dilemma occurs because Lauren has never developed systems that are designed around how SHE thinks. And yes, believe it or not, there is a system lurking out there in this universe for every person reading this book...including YOU!

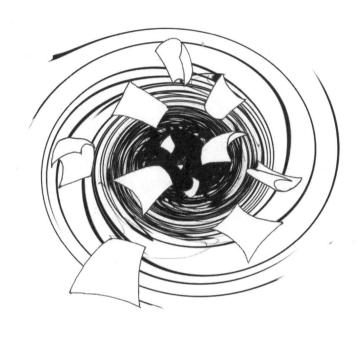

Belief Tune-Up

You believe that you can't put things away because, in the past, you've had no systems that would help you believe otherwise. To change that belief, you simply need to listen to yourself (or a professional organizer) to learn and understand your thought process and what will work for you. This is what makes or breaks a system. NOTE: There is nothing wrong with papers or items being out in the open, as long as you are happy with that location becoming a permanent home for your items. If you are trying to *de*clutter, this idea may not be conducive to your goal.

Some tools can help you change your beliefs. For papers, a tool you can use is the PaperConnect™ Tickler File. This system helps you to make decisions and becomes a home for your papers until you need to act on them. This is covered in Chapter 10.

Another tool that remedies this excuse is the creation of an index for items or papers so that you know where things are located. This is covered in Chapter 12.

☐ 6. ORGANIZING AND CREATIVITY DON'T MIX.

If you are creative, I will grant you that the right side of your brain may be more active than the left. However, you still need focus and clarity in order to be successful in your creativity. Don't you think that being surrounded by clutter (also known as piles of stress) inhibits your ability to create freely?

Belief Tune-Up

First, you must believe that clutter crushes your creativity. Until you grasp that, you are fighting an uphill battle. Second, invest the time to clear your workspace and have fewer items, both physically and mentally, in your way. The doors to creativity will not only open up, but they will be wider! So stop stewing over the clutter, wasting hours each day beating yourself up about how disorganized you are, or feeling stymied because you can't produce good work due to a mental block. Once you are organized, you will have additional time and energy to exercise your creative genius more effectively.

☐ 7. YOU DON'T THINK ORGANIZING IS EXCITING.

I won't take it personally if you think that organizing is dull, but let me tell you that it doesn't have to be! If you'd rather put a sharp stick in your eye than get organized, simply change the beliefs that you have in your head. You will see your behavior soon follow.

 **Belief Tune-Up**

With simple processes and built-in rewards that you will learn from this book, you will find that organizing can be both easy and fun. If you know there is something waiting for you at the end of an organizing session, it can be very motivating. Using some creativity, organizing can take on a whole new light.

Here's how: promise yourself that AFTER you organize your closet for 2 hours (or whatever amount of time you have), you can do something that appeals to you—take a walk, read your favorite novel, go golfing, take a bubble bath, get an ice cream cone, refill your coffee cup, reread this book. Remember the reward is to FOLLOW the organizing session, not precede it.

Believing that you will get to the reward helps you stick to your plan by keeping the end in mind. You will see progress and be motivated like never before. *Believe* me!

Patty Kreamer

Another idea is to have a *clutter buddy*. A clutter buddy is someone that will help motivate you to keep going and who can alleviate any boredom that may set in. Take turns helping each other and you will both learn from the experience on each end.

If you look at organizing as a boring or grueling chore, you'll hate every minute of it. Envision the end results—no more stress, no more piles, setting a good example for others, being able to find things when you need them and not by accident 3 weeks later!

☐ 8. YOU'VE ALWAYS DONE IT THAT WAY.

This is an old cop-out and it certainly suggests a lack of desire to change. Just because you've always done it that way doesn't mean it is the best way of doing it. Consider that there may be a better way of doing something, and give yourself the freedom to explore.

Belief Tune-Up

"My way or the highway" is a pretty narrow-minded notion. If, instead, you are receptive to new ideas and you give them a chance, you may find that there is a better way. Change is not always easy, but in many cases, it can improve efficiency and quality of life. Looking for a better way and being open to suggestions can invite new ideas and opportunities.

Review some of your practices. If you do something just because your parents or grandparents did (keep every torn shirt, worn pair of pants, mismatched sock, pay stub, electric bill, newspaper, recipe, old winter coat, broken lamp, shopping bag, twisty tie, rubber band, glass jar, plastic container, purse, blanket, towel, appliance), it doesn't mean that you have to keep doing it forever.

Review Excuses #1 and #2 above for more Belief Tune-Ups.

REVIEW

EXCUSES—can be corrected by changing your attitude or **beliefs.**

1. But you might need it someday!
2. You can't throw anything away.
3. You are a true perfectionist.
4. You are afraid you'll fail.
5. If you can't see it, you forget it.
6. Organizing and creativity don't mix.
7. You don't think organizing is exciting.
8. You've always done it that way.

_____
_____
_____
_____
_____
_____
_____
_____
_____
_____
_____
_____
_____
_____
_____
_____
_____
_____

"Never allow force of habit to block a better way."

Maria Gracia
www.getorganizednow.com

CHAPTER FOUR:

Obstacles

...An obstacle can be corrected by changing your behavior.

1. You just have too much stuff!
2. Your stuff needs a home.
3. You have no time to clean up.
4. You have the wrong type of storage.
5. You inherited systems or items.
6. You were never taught how to organize.
7. You grew up with clutter.
8. You find comfort in clutter.
9. You're a P-r-o-c-r-a-s-t-i-n-a-t-o-r.
10. You don't set goals or priorities.

1. YOU JUST HAVE TOO MUCH STUFF!

We are living in the best economic times in history, which means that we have more items at our fingertips than ever before. Everything is available to satiate our "instant gratification" attitude. In other words, if we want it, we get it.

However, there is a penalty to pay for such behavior. No matter how much stuff you have, you still only have so much time in your day to indulge yourself, and so much space in which to store everything. If half of your clutter disappeared, you would still have more than enough things to keep you active—I guarantee it!

 **Behavior Tune-Up**

Excessive shopping (a.k.a. The Enemy) is a behavior that can be truly detrimental to an organized life. In fact, it can be detrimental to more than just an organized life. It can deplete your wallet, increase your stress, and consume your time. So how do you get around shopping fever?

SCENARIO: Ted is in the store debating whether to buy *another* set of golf clubs. Actually, for Ted, there is no debate; he just knows that he is going to buy them. STOP RIGHT THERE, TED! This is where Ted needs to ask himself the following (dreaded) question...Do I WANT these golf clubs or do I NEED these golf clubs?

If Ted WANTS golf clubs, he should walk away (Go, Ted, Go!) and agree that he will come back in a week and buy them if he absolutely must. The best part is that there is a 90% chance that Ted will forget about them and live happily ever after with his old golf clubs. Impulse buying can lead to clutter beyond your wildest nightmares.

If Ted NEEDS golf clubs, then buying them may be justified, but only if Ted is sure that he has a place to store them before he does. Example: Ted has a golf outing tomorrow and his old golf clubs were crushed when his partner ran them over with a golf cart and nobody he knows has a set of left-handed clubs that he can borrow on such short notice. (Ted may also want to consider the NEED for getting another golf partner!)

The results from this change in behavior can be dramatic. If you really intend to change your behavior, you will not only see a decrease in clutter but you will save money as well!

Need some help in digesting this behavior change? Try using the "One in—one out" rule. If you buy a new blouse, you must get rid of one (gasp!). If you buy a new pair of shoes, you must toss an old pair. This helps to decrease the clutter build-up. If you want to declutter your life more quickly, use the "One in—two out (or –three out or –four out)" rule. The higher the number, the more quickly the clutter will go away.

☐ 2. YOUR STUFF NEEDS A HOME.

If you invited me to your house, could you find me a spoon? The answer (I hope) is OF COURSE! Whether you moved into your home 3 days or 3 decades ago, one of the first and automatic things that you do is assign a drawer for silverware. Sure your spoons go on vacations—they go to the table, the dishwasher, or the living room, but they always seem to find their way back home. This is not true of the items that you call clutter, many of which you use every day. How often do you have to search for stamps? Scissors? Tape? Labels? Glasses? Keys? Wallet? Files? Important documents? Need I go on?

 **Behavior Tune-Up**

Here's the secret—instead of throwing things down and being happy with where they land, take the time to assign a permanent home for the aforementioned items and any other stray objects that seem to have legs of their own. To assign a permanent home should take no more than a minute or two, and it's time well spent. You will save so much time and energy looking for things and you will decrease your stress level while you are at it!

Your habits can guide you in assigning a home for certain items. For example, if Kim can never find her watch in the morning, she needs to make a ritual of taking off her jewelry at night. She should choose a logical place that she can take off her watch *each* night so she can find it in the same place *each* morning. Routines can make a positive difference in your life without being boring. You have the power and freedom to make decisions on where things should go, so why not exercise them?

☐ 3. YOU HAVE NO TIME TO CLEAN UP.

Let's say that you have taken the time to assign homes and you know where things belong. The problem is that you never seem to have time to put things away. Perhaps you are over-scheduling yourself, leaving no time to clean up and put things back in their home when you are done using them.

"Let your involvement be determined by your goals, not by your availability."

— Author unknown

Behavior Tune-Up

Congratulations! You are halfway there if you have assigned homes for your most sought-after items. The next step is to change the way you manage your time. When scheduling your tasks, be sure to include a REALISTIC time frame that includes clean up, travel time, last minute matters, etc. If Wendy normally takes one hour to pay her bills but never has time to put the checkbook, envelopes, and stamps away, she should schedule one hour and fifteen minutes to do the job. Wendy should not PLAN on doing anything else until the job is completed and everything has found its way home. For a great way to enhance your time management skills when organizing, see the HALF-TIME rule in Chapter 7.

☐ 4. YOU HAVE THE WRONG TYPE OF STORAGE.

This can mean many things, not the least of which is broken or defective storage. For example, if Danell has a file cabinet that is difficult to use (the drawers stick or don't open all the way), she is not likely to file her papers on a regular basis. Another type of incorrect storage can be a cute storage container that you bought on impulse—a clutterer's major foe. Once you get it back to the house or office, you set it down, maybe attempt to use it, and realize that it has no place in your life (but it is *so* cute). Slowly, you realize that it wasn't what you NEEDED but rather what you WANTED. By now, you have lost the receipt and figure "...BUT I MIGHT NEED IT SOME DAY," so you stick it in a closet or the garage or basement. That storage container now becomes new clutter.

I can just see you shaking your head, wondering how I know this has happened to you. This is not an uncommon occurrence.

Behavior Tune-Up

Be sure to have working storage options. Danell needs to invest $100 in a quality file cabinet. It is worth the money to relieve the stress of looking at piles of unfiled paperwork!

Try to avoid using storage that will involve another step in the organizing process. For example, if you are going to use containers that stack, be sure that you have easy in-and-out access. Inevitably, the one that you need is always at the bottom of the stack, which may make using it inconvenient. To sidestep this problem, build shelves to house each container.

Another way to avoid having the wrong type of storage is to know what you need *before* you go to the store.

☐ 5. YOU INHERITED SYSTEMS OR ITEMS.

Very rarely do you find two people that think alike, so what are the chances of you moving in on someone else's territory and matching their thought process? If you have ever been lucky enough to take over someone's position at work, then you know what I am talking about. What's worse is that when you take over the space, there is usually no time to reorganize the files, furniture, or overall systems to suit your needs. You are expected to get right to the job at hand without a grace period to design and implement new systems for you. Usually, about 6-12 months into the job, you are buried in papers and general clutter with no place to put them because the space is still full of your predecessor's stuff—and you have never even looked at his stuff!

Divorce, illness or death of a loved one, or combining households after marriage can create a similar situation at home. Part of the difficulty of dealing with inherited items is the feeling that you *have* to keep them all. Those feelings are very real, but they can be overcome.

 **Behavior Tune-Up**

Pause. Whether it is at home or at the office, this often-overlooked behavior can add perspective. If you stop for a short while to assess the situation, even if you have to do so on your time off, you will find it to be a worthwhile investment.

Take the time to declutter the area in which you will work before you start. This will produce the feeling of a clean, fresh beginning that is custom-made just for you.

To be successful, you need to schedule time to organize the inherited space, papers, and items in general. Don't just say you will do it or put it on your to-do list. Instead, put it in your day planner on a specific date and time. You will be more likely to do it if you schedule it rather than thinking or saying you'll do it.

For inherited items at home, this is closely related to sentimentality, which is covered in Chapter 5.

☐ 6. YOU WERE NEVER TAUGHT ORGANIZATION.

We are taught many things in school but organizing is not usually one of them. I have yet to find Organizing 101 in schools or colleges. Our upbringing and education have a lot to do with how organized or disorganized we are as adults.

Behavior Tune-Up

Often it is assumed that we know how to organize our lives, when, for many, it is not a natural ability, but rather a learned skill. So the best news of all is that you can learn to be organized, just like you can learn to ride a bike! As you read this book, you are educating yourself on how to get organized! Most of the answers are right in your hands now. Recognizing the need for help in organizing is important, because it opens your mind to ideas that may work for you.

If you want the personal attention of a professional organizer, visit www.napo.net to find a professional organizer in your area and see if you can meet with him or her. Professional organizing is a full-blown industry, and many businesses are at your service.

You may want to attend a class or seminar presented by a professional organizer in your area. Check with your community college and local associations to see if they offer classes or programs on getting organized.

☐ 7. YOU GREW UP WITH CLUTTER.

If you grew up in a cluttered environment, chances are you will carry that with you and unfortunately, pass it on to your children. On the other hand, a cluttered childhood can have the opposite effect on some people— they grow up and rebel and become the neatniks of the world. A cluttered environment is the last way that they want to live.

Behavior Tune-Up

The first step in breaking the clutter cycle is to look at the premise of your behavior and question it *before* accepting it as being cast in stone. Does living with clutter make it right just because that was how you grew up? Probably not.

The clutter in your life is usually directly related to your behavior, and your behavior is often linked to your upbringing. In other words, your upbringing has an impact on many of the decisions that you make consciously and subconsciously throughout your life.

For example, if Lee grew up in a home where the dirty laundry was thrown on the floor until she was asked to bring it to the laundry room on laundry day, then she routinely lived amongst piles of clothes on the floor. Maybe hampers or laundry bags were never used in Lee's home. Therefore, Lee may carry on the same tradition as she goes out on her own, never considering the possibility of using the aforementioned tools.

Make an effort to talk to people in your life besides family members to gather some different ideas that maybe you never thought of doing. It's also a good idea to visit stores that carry organizing products. See the Resources in the Appendix for more ideas.

☐ 8. YOU FIND COMFORT IN CLUTTER.

Your upbringing may play a role in this obstacle as well. If you grew up in a household that hoarded things of little value, you may have what I call the "Depression mentality." I believe that there was value during the Depression in keeping things like glass jars, rubber bands, twisty ties, plastic and paper bags, used envelopes, tin foil, etc., but nowadays, hoarding is rarely necessary. Contrary to popular belief, club membership to warehouse-type stores does not require that you keep a one-year supply of anything, including toilet paper, soap, paper towels, shampoo, etc. You may save money, but you lose your valuable space to storage, and you lose your peace of mind by having extra supplies to trip over all the time.

Hoarding for some creates a sense of security. Perhaps you feel safer and more in control when you are surrounded by lots of stuff. If this is the case, you may want to start small by clearing out just one room to see what it is like to live without your things crowding you. You might realize that you prefer that freedom to the cramped feeling you have lived with for so long.

Behavior Tune-Up

The best way to start to control clutter is to stop bringing things into your life! Refrain from going on shopping sprees, especially to the warehouse-type stores, and loading up on things for which you really have no room. And the only garage sale that I recommend that you go to is your own.

If the stuff that you already have can be used, consider keeping it ONLY if you plan on using it in the near future. There is no need to keep things that you will NEVER use. Ask yourself if you are keeping too many of an item. After all, how many twisty-ties can a person use in her lifetime?

☐ 9. YOU'RE A P-R-O-C-R-A-S-T-I-N-A-T-O-R!

I was going to procrastinate and save this for last, but I wanted to change my behavior! Procrastination has caused many people to lose sleep, money, happiness and more, not only from worry, but also from having to finish doing things at the last minute. The big question is why do we do it? The answer can be simple: it's easier *not* to do the task. Or it can be more complex: rather than feeling overwhelmed, you are **not** going to think about the task until the last minute.

There is a lot of psychology behind procrastination, and since I don't claim to be a psychologist, I will stick to the simplistic way of handling it. Here are four obstacles surrounding procrastination and their solutions.

 **Behavior Tune-Up**

It is easier NOT to do something than it is to do it. If you are a person who likes to make to-do lists (either in your head or on paper), you may look up and down your list and gravitate towards the easier tasks that are not nearly as high priority. It's easy to scan right over the less-than-attractive tasks. Solution? Schedule *all* of your to-do items in specific time slots in your day planner or Personal Digital Assistant (e.g. Palm™ Handheld). A much higher percentage of tasks will be checked off at the end of the day.

Usually we put off the things that we do not like to do, are not good at, don't really know how to do, or that seem unimportant to us. Simply put, this is human nature. If you find yourself pushing a to-do forward day after day, confront it. Ask yourself if there is someone else that could or would do it for you. If it is something that you just are not good at, maybe you should consider educating yourself in that area so it is not such a big deal every time it arises. For example, if you have to turn in an expense report and crunching numbers is not your thing, find someone that loves math and ask if they'll do your report for you. Barter by offering to do something for them that they don't like doing. Or ask others how they do their reports—there might be a better or easier way of which you are unaware.

The task or project seems SOOOO overwhelming. You have a huge project that is going to take 30 hours to do and you have six months to do it. That sixth month is here before you know it and you are scrambling to get it all done. This is *not* healthy. Instead of looking at it as a 30-hour project, look at it as six 5-hour projects. That means you only have to spend five hours per month over the next six months!

71

That is much more do-able. Go even further by breaking the five-hours per month into five 1-hour projects and schedule each one-hour chunk into time slots in your day planner or PDA. Doesn't that project seem much more manageable now?

You don't know where to start. In looking at a 30-hour project, finding a starting point can be tricky. Say you had to eat a hippopotamus (what are the odds?) Would you eat it all in one chunk? No, of course not—you would take small chunks, one at time. That's exactly how you break down a big project. List all of the chunks (steps) and then schedule one chunk at a time. For example, if Nadalie wants to organize her whole office (very overwhelming), she needs to start by narrowing it down to her desk, and then choosing a specific drawer. That will get her started. She would then move on to the next drawer, then to the top of the desk, and so on in little chunks.

So go on, start organizing your bedroom or office, or begin that project that is not due for 3 more months. Get a head start...you'll be glad that you did!

By the way, I was going to make an illustration for procrastination but I kept putting it off. ☺

☐ 10. YOU DON'T SET GOALS OR PRIORITIES.

Starting out on a path without knowing where it leads is adventuresome. But do you really want finding your car keys to be an adventure every day? Goal setting may seem trite but it is VITAL for success in any capacity of life, and getting organized is no exception. You need a picture in your mind of your desired results so you may start on the right path and end up in the right place.

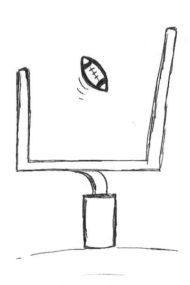

> *"Goal setting starts with a pad of paper, a pen and you."*

Gary Ryan Blair, Personal Coach

 **Behavior Tune-Up**

Take an hour of your time to create a vision of what you want to accomplish. Set goals that will help you achieve that vision. Then list the tasks or steps that you need to take in order to meet your goals. Don't just say or think your goals. **Write them down.** There is something magical about writing your goals on paper. It seals them in your subconscious as real and obtainable. If you don't believe me, TRY IT! Here are some tips on goal setting.

THINK AHEAD IN REVERSE (HUH?)

Imagine that it is a year from today and write yourself a letter describing what you have accomplished in the past year and how you did it. Think about what you want your overall achievements to be for the next year. In other words, see what you want and work backwards! If you want to make lifetime goals, write your obituary. I know that sounds morbid, but what do you want to have accomplished and what do you want people to say about you when you are gone?

BE S.M.A.R.T.

Any goal that you set should have 5 characteristics. They should be:

S = Specific
M = Measurable
A = Achievable
R = Realistic
T = Time related

Whether short-term or long-term, if your goal is not S.M.A.R.T., it isn't complete and may go unaccomplished. For example, if your goal is to be rich, you are being too vague. But if you write down that you want to earn $80,000 by 12/31 of the current year, it is starting to fit the SMART model. It's Specific and Measurable ($80,000), and it is Time related (by12/31). Whether it is Achievable and Realistic, only you would know.

SHARE YOUR VISION

Don't keep your goals a secret. Share them with the important people in your life so that they can keep you on track and hold you accountable. In fact, finding someone that has goals and talking with them once a month to be sure that you are both staying focused is a great way to make goal setting fun and effective.

By the way, only 3% of the population writes down their goals. They happen to be the most happy, healthy, and successful people on the planet. Coincidence? I don't think so.

REVIEW

OBSTACLES—An obstacle can be corrected by changing your **behavior**.

1. You just have too much stuff!
2. Your stuff needs a home.
3. You have no time to clean up.
4. You have the wrong type of storage.
5. You inherited systems or items.
6. You were never taught organization.
7. You grew up with clutter.
8. You find comfort in clutter.
9. You're a P-r-o-c-r-a-s-t-i-n-a-t-o-r.
10. You don't set goals or priorities.

_____
_____
_____
_____
_____
_____
_____
_____
_____
_____
_____
_____
_____
_____
_____
_____
_____
_____

*"An optimist sees an opportunity in every
calamity; a pessimist sees a calamity in every
opportunity."*

- Winston Churchill, British Statesman

CHAPTER FIVE:

Reasons

...A reason is possibly correctable, but it may
be out of your control to do so.

1. You have too much to do!
2. You don't have enough space.
3. You remain after a downsizing.
4. You deal with difficult people.
5. You are very sentimental.
6. You experience a life-changing event.

☐ 1. YOU HAVE TOO MUCH TO DO.

With fast-paced days full of work, errands, running the kids to and from extracurricular activities, making meals, paying bills, and on and on, when do you have time to do it all? The problem is...you don't.

 **ADJUSTMENTS**

LEARN TO SAY NO – Accept that you just can't do everything that either you'd like to do or that people ask of you. As Harold Taylor said, "Separate the person from the talk. You are saying no to a job, not trying to hurt a person, so don't feel guilty. Be brief or you may find yourself giving in. Offer an explanation, not an excuse."

People generally understand if you give them a reasonable explanation. If you tell a lie, it is usually obvious that you are trying to get out of something and it almost always comes back to bite you. The fact of the matter is that no one should have to give a reason for saying no, except maybe to a boss (or spouse—ouch!)

A good all-purpose way to decline a new task request is, "I'd love to, but I just can't take on any more tasks right now." If someone else is available and suitable for the task, you may want to say, "I am unable to do this for you now, but check with Jack in accounting." Unless you are in a position of authority, though, you may want to check with Jack before you offer his services.

If you find yourself with more and more responsibilities on your plate, try keeping a daily log sheet for a week on an hour-by-hour basis. It is best to do so from a Wednesday to a Wednesday—this gives the flavor from 2 different weeks and may offer a more comprehensive look at your daily activities.

If this is work related, see how your days unfold, and notice what gets done and what does not. Then approach your manager and show her the results of the log. If everything on your plate was high priority, you need to let her know that you are only able to accomplish so much. Ask her to be more specific about what is most important.

If this is not work related, share the information with the people in your life that are demanding your time. Let them know how you think your time would be better spent.

This tracking log can also be a wake up call for you. You may discover that you do waste a lot of time and you need to plan your days more judiciously. Planning is the key to any successful day. If you let the emergencies of others control your day, you will accomplish fewer of your own tasks. How do you effectively deal with the emergencies of others?

1. Define what NOW means. Many times when someone calls you or comes to you and says that they need it done now (because it's convenient for them), it doesn't necessarily mean immediately. They might mean in the next week or so. Ask.

2. Make yourself accessible only at certain times of the day. If someone has a question and you are not available, he will normally find the answers on his own.

DAILY ACTIVITY LOG SHEET
Date_____

TIME	ACTIVITY
8:00	
8:30	
9:00	
9:30	
10:00	
10:30	
11:00	
11:30	
12:00	
12:30	
1:00	
1:30	
2:00	
2:30	
3:00	
3:30	
4:00	
4:30	
5:00	
5:30	
6:00	
6:30	
7:00	
7:30	
8:00	

3. Try to refrain from being the resource center where everyone comes when they need something. Let someone else do that.

Now, back to planning your day. If you take just 10-20 minutes at the beginning or end of the day to plan, you will be amazed at how much more effective you will be.

For every one minute that you plan, you can save up to twelve minutes. So if you plan for just 10 minutes a day, that may give you up to two full hours of productive time!

As you map out your time, you may also recognize those tasks that don't need to be done, are redundant, or can be delegated. The result: you will finally find some time for YOU!

2. YOU DON'T HAVE ENOUGH SPACE.

This is something that may be out of your control at work or at home. If you work in a cubicle, you must use the space as sensibly as possible. At home, a bigger home or an addition is not always in the cards.

Patty Kreamer

 **ADJUSTMENTS**

If purchasing more space is not an option, the first step is to purge the space that you do have. If you have file cabinets or storage areas around you, evaluate them to see if you can purge them and/or archive the contents. For papers, such as bills, receipts, investment statements, cancelled checks, or bank statements, I recommend that you speak to your accountant or lawyer to know what you must keep and what can be thrown away. If you have kept items like your cable bills or gas and electric bills for years, you

84

are most likely wasting your effort. How often do you refer to them? If never, throw them out!

As mentioned earlier, if there is a question about your bill, normally the utility company can provide archived copies for you (call first to be sure, but let *them* keep the records). Be sure you are keeping these papers for good reason. If, of course, you write off your utilities for tax purposes, that would be a good reason to keep them for as long as your accountant recommends.

Of the papers that you are keeping, ask yourself what can be kept off-site or away from your home or work area. We will discuss solutions to this problem in Chapter 12.

With items other than papers, such as your personal belongings, clothes, toys, etc., the same principle applies.

☆ Can you throw some of it away because it is no longer useful to you or anyone else?
☆ If you do have to keep it, can it be stored elsewhere so that you have room for what you need now?
☆ Can you donate some items?

By asking these questions, you can use the space that you have most effectively. GET THE URGE TO PURGE!

☐ 3. YOU REMAIN AFTER A DOWNSIZING.

Downsizing is difficult for the person that has to leave, but it can also be difficult for the people that remain. The downsize survivors have their own work to do, and then they get buried under someone else's duties as well. To make matters worse, the departed person's organizing systems probably don't make much sense to the inheritor. The workload and confusion can be absolutely overwhelming!

 **ADJUSTMENTS**

If you find yourself in this situation, you may have some options. If you have an understanding boss with whom you can communicate, track what you do on a daily basis for at least a week and then show him what you are capable of doing or not doing. (See Daily Activity Log Sheet.) Ask your supervisor what his priorities are so that you are not concentrating on low priority items.

For more adjustments that are related to inheriting someone else's systems, refer to Chapter 4.

☐ 4. YOU DEAL WITH DIFFICULT PEOPLE.

This is a favorite of mine, because no matter who I talk to, the difficult person is always the one who is not present to defend himself. But if you are in this situation, there is a simple way out (NOTE: I didn't say easy).

 **ADJUSTMENTS**

Meet with the difficult person or persons in your life. Maybe they don't understand the way that you think about organization. They put things in one place that makes no sense to you, and you put them in another that makes no sense to them. At this meeting, use the following three steps to solve this problem.

Step 1. Negotiate and develop the new rules until everyone is in agreement. (The scissors always go in the top left hand drawer of your desk when not in use.)

Step 2. Convey those rules to those expected to abide by them (family meeting, word of mouth, email, memo, announcement, etc.).

Step 3. Live with them!

Again, it sounds simple (and it is) but it's not necessarily easy because people aren't always so quick to compromise. Of course, that is part of the negotiating process.

Make sure that you build in rewards and consequences for those that do and do not follow the new rules. For example, whoever doesn't put the scissors back in the drawer has to put a quarter in a jar (consequence). When there is enough money in the jar, you can use that money to buy lunch for everyone, even those that did not break the rule (reward)!

☐ 5.   YOU ARE VERY SENTIMENTAL.

Sentimentality was always tough for me to grasp...until my parents recently moved. I am the fifth of five children, and I always joke that there are a total of 2 pictures of me from birth to now (which isn't too far off!) By the time parents get to kid #5, they've "been there, done that." So sentimentality was not engraved on my psyche at any age. But when my parents recently moved, I got a first hand look at how hard it is to let go of items that have memories attached. And yes, I came home with memorabilia that I never knew existed, but I only took something if I knew I had a place for it and if I had a use for it!

Patty Kreamer

 **ADJUSTMENTS**

Sentimentality can mask itself as an excuse or a reason. What this means is that you may have the power to change your beliefs in this area and be less sentimental. But for many of you, your roots are very engrained and there is no letting go of your beliefs. Therefore, sentimentality is a *reason* for keeping things.

In Chapter 3, we said that a good place to start is to make sure that you are keeping only those items that have GOOD memories attached to them. Why keep items that make you feel badly? It takes enormous amounts of energy to hold onto bad memories. So if you think someone else in the family would be better off keeping the items that stir up negative memories, pass them on. Otherwise, you may want to consider selling, donating, or throwing these items away.

If an item evokes good memories and you really want to declutter, take a picture of it. Better yet, a camcorder allows you to talk about the memories attached as you pan across many items that you are getting rid of. Stored properly in albums, in cabinets, or on shelves, photos and video tapes take up much less space and can provide the same kind of memory. In fact, you might consider them better than the original item because you can view them without going to the attic or basement to dig out heavy boxes or trunks that smell like mildew!

6. YOU EXPERIENCE A LIFE-CHANGING EVENT.

Life happens all the time, but sometimes events occur that make organizing take a backseat to what is happening now. Events like:

☆ Planning a wedding
☆ Getting married
☆ Getting divorced
☆ Buying or selling a home
☆ Moving
☆ Becoming a parent
☆ Sending a child off to college
☆ The illness or death of a loved one
☆ Losing a job
☆ Starting a new job
☆ Changing hours of work
☆ Taking a long vacation

When these big events hit, we are not always prepared for the aftermath. Our usual systems fall apart and we are greeted with clutter problems as the event concludes.

 **ADJUSTMENTS**

Recognize that as an event or situation unfolds, it is likely that things may get out of hand and that organization may not be a priority. By recognizing this, you may be able to prepare in advance so that the results aren't as debilitating in the end.

93

Plan ahead. Make a plan to deal with the event so that fewer surprises come your way. If you are planning a wedding, I hear there are many things to consider. I wouldn't know first hand, as George and I got married in Las Vegas. Our wedding took one phone call to plan and cost a total of $65.09 (including the limo, flowers, music, and trip to the courthouse for our marriage license. Little White Chapel has cornered the market for simple nuptials!)

If you plan on getting married in a more traditional way, it will help you to:

☆ Set goals
☆ Create timelines
☆ Make checklists
☆ Assign tasks to others involved
☆ Schedule when tasks should be done

These are all effective planning tools. If you plan successfully, you will have much less "clean up" in the end.

What if you can't plan? When life catches you by surprise, what can you do? First, you can turn to your family and friends for support. Second, now may be a good time to call in a professional organizer to expedite the recovery process. An organizer will be adept at handling these situations and can assist you in a clearer and quicker resolution to the disorganization. At the very least, an organizer can provide you with a way to get started and help you make a plan to reach your desired goals.

REVIEW

REASONS—possibly correctible, but it may be out of your control to do so.

1. You have too much to do!
2. You don't have enough space.
3. You remain after a downsizing.
4. You deal with difficult people.
5. You are very sentimental.
6. You experience a life-changing event.

_____
_____
_____
_____
_____
_____
_____
_____
_____
_____
_____
_____
_____
_____
_____
_____
_____
_____

"Most people never run far enough on their first wind to find out if they've got a second. Give your dreams all you've got, and you'll be amazed at the energy that comes out of you."

William James

CHAPTER SIX:

<u>READY</u> to wrap it up

You have read 24 stumbling blocks that inhibit organization—8 excuses, 10 obstacles, and 6 reasons. This is by no means to be considered a comprehensive list. You may have some areas of your life that don't fall neatly into the excuses, obstacles, and reasons that were listed. If this is the case, look at your own situation and ask WHY? If you question the premise, you can usually get to the root of the problem more quickly.

WHEW! WHAT DOES IT ALL MEAN?

GETTING READY can be tiring, but it is critical and worthwhile if you want long-lasting results. You should be proud of yourself for making it this far. After reading the many excuses, obstacles, and reasons that may cause disorganization, you should have a better understanding of:

☆ What's keeping you from getting organized

☆ Why your attempts at getting organized in the past may have been less than successful

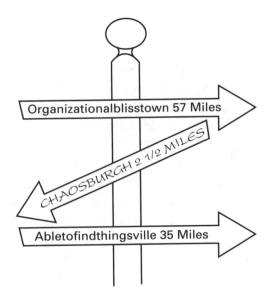

NOW WHAT?

Now that you have a better handle on your clutter challenges and some ideas on how you can overcome them, it's time to face them head on.

If you have concluded that you are **READY** to conquer your clutter and get organized once and for all, then let's get **SET!**

NOTE: If you feel you are not yet ready or comfortable getting organized on your own, now would be a good time to contact a professional organizer near you for a personal consultation. I would suggest that you finish reading this book first, though, before you do.

Visit the National Association of Professional Organizers website at www.napo.net or the Professional Organizers Web Ring website at www.organizerswebring.com for an organizer referral in your area.

Patty Kreamer

PART I READY

EXERCISE

Why is it important for me to get organized?

_____

_____

_____

_____

_____

_____

_____

What excuses, obstacles, or reasons are keeping me from getting organized?

_____

_____

_____

_____

_____

_____

_____

What can I do to overcome them?

_____

_____

_____

_____

_____

_____

_____

Am I ready to get organized now?

☐ Absolutely!

☐ Sure, why not?

☐ Not sure yet. I think I need to review what I've read so far.

☐ Nope, not yet, but I will continue reading and hope that I can find the oomph that I need.

IMPORTANT NOTE: Whatever is causing you to be disorganized now may be correctable, but conditions will change as your life changes. You may be creative and cluttered today and overcome it tomorrow. In two years, however, you'll have a whole new set of circumstances that may cause disorganization. For example, if you have a child, you may find that you are becoming disorganized again, but in a different way and for different reasons. At that time, revisit this book and repeat this exercise.

REVIEW

Ready to wrap it up
Whew! What does it all mean?

☆ What's keeping you from getting organized.
☆ Why your attempts at getting organized in the past may have been less than successful.

Now what?
Part I Exercise

_____
_____
_____
_____
_____
_____
_____
_____
_____
_____
_____
_____
_____
_____
_____
_____
_____
_____
_____

PART II: SET...

> *"'On course' doesn't mean perfect. 'On course' means that even when things don't go perfectly - you are still going in the right direction."*
>
> *Charles Garfield, Author*

CHAPTER SEVEN:

SET...

If you ask me, I'd say that getting READY in Part 1 is probably the most exhausting of the 3 steps to getting organized, and you haven't even picked up one piece of clutter yet! However, all three steps are equally important, and now that you are in Part II, you are one third of the way to getting successfully organized!

In Chapter 2, we looked at the Circle of Change that includes the three components needed in order for change to take place in your life:

☆ **Beliefs**
☆ **Behaviors**
☆ **Tools**

Since then, you have taken an intense look *into* yourself—more specifically your **beliefs** and **behavior**—to discover what has contributed to or has caused your disorganization. Now, I am going to ask you to take a look *around* you.

LOOK AROUND AT YOUR SPACE

The physical features of the space that you inhabit have great impact on your success at getting organized. As you look around at your physical space, you will be identifying problem areas as well as those features that work well. To adequately evaluate your environment and implement change, you will need to learn new **TOOLS.** When I talk about **TOOLS,** I am referring to the techniques I use to create and implement organizing systems.

READY TO GET SET

Perhaps the most important tool we will use to get organized is a **PLAN**.

WHAT'S IN A PLAN?

☆ A decided activity for the room
☆ A lot o' logic
☆ A drawing
☆ A list of what you'll need
☆ A realistic time schedule
☆ An urge to purge

You are literally going to "set the scene" by creating a map or drawing of your space as it exists now and as you'd like it to be. Your plan will also include a step-by-step plan of action with specific times scheduled for each activity. You wouldn't build an airplane— commercial or model—without step-by-step instructions on how to complete the project. The same goes for getting organized. You need to map out your plan.

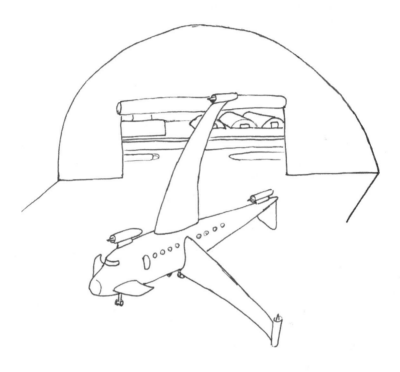

With no plan, you are more likely to fail at long-term organizing results. Just like the scenario in the beginning of this book, the room or area that you clean up will be back to its original messy state if you don't think the plan all the way through.

A plan is necessary no matter what area you are working in—office, garage, basement, bedroom, kitchen, bathroom, car, linen closet, or any area that needs to be organized. You shouldn't just blindly start to put things away and expect the area to stay that way.

For example, say Diane moved into someone else's office when she got her new job. She didn't have the time to "set up shop" or think about how she wanted to arrange things because she had to get right to work. Shuffling the furniture to function for her and the way she worked was not possible.

The sad part about this scenario is that a personalized office setup is vital to your productivity and efficiency. What worked for Diane's predecessor will not likely work for Diane in the long run. Take the time to look around before you make any big move. What can you change without much effort to suit your needs? What is obviously out of place? What preferences can you incorporate quickly?

A DECIDED ACTIVITY FOR THE ROOM

Before you do anything, you need to determine exactly what activities will take place in the room in which you are organizing. For example, you have an extra bedroom that is currently being used as your dumping ground for everything without a home, and you are tired of wasting the valuable space. Maybe you want to convert it to a sewing room, a reading room, an office, a storage room, or an art room. Knowing what the room will be used for is critical. Allow for the fact that an area may have more than one decided activity. Since not everyone has the luxury of having a room for each and every activity in their life, you might designate one room to serve as your reading and sewing room. Once you know the room's purpose, you should only allow items into the room that pertain to these decided activities.

A LOT O' LOGIC!

As you look at the space, be sure that whatever furniture, equipment, or fixtures you keep are placed logically in the room. It would not make sense to put a magazine rack where you have to get up to use it; instead, put it next to the recliner that you sit in to read. Don't put a file cabinet in a place that is difficult to access; you will be less likely to file and soon your files will become piles.

One of my clients, Gayle, had her chair up against a wall with her desk in front of her (as shown below). Around her desk were old file cabinets (OFC's) with old files, while her current file cabinets (CFC's) were out in the hallway! Gayle also had bookcases (BC's) across from the old file cabinets that blocked her pathway to her chair. She had to literally turn sideways to get to her desk! The table and chairs were used as a catchall because it was awkward to sit there so far from her phone and computer.

BEFORE

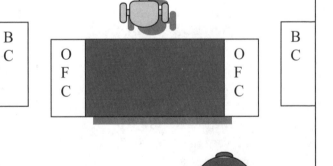

Needless to say, Gayle didn't file much because filing was inconvenient, not to mention unappealing. So we turned her desk around to face the wall, took the old file cabinets (OFC's) out and put the current file cabinets (CFC's) in her office.

AFTER

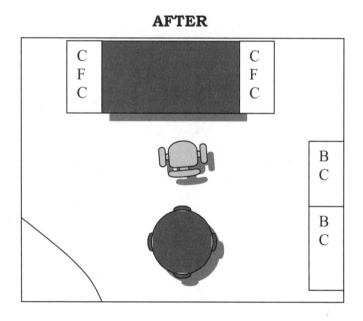

Now the wall did not cramp her, she was able to file because the current file cabinets were within reach, and the openness created a more inviting atmosphere. In addition, Gayle no longer had to squeeze between the file cabinets and bookcases (BC's) to sit behind her desk. Since she didn't use most of the books on a daily basis, we moved the bookcases (BC's) away from her, keeping those she referred to often on the shelves closest to her. We moved the table and chairs to create a reading and research area that she could use with the turn of her chair. The difference in her productivity was like night and day, and all it took was a little planning, time, and logic!

A DRAWING

As you see in the above example, a drawing can be very helpful. Your drawing doesn't need to be beautiful or exact. It needs to be just good enough to show walls, doors windows so you can plan around them.

Make a drawing of the room as it is now, and one that shows where you want things to go. Think through how YOU will function in the room, and design the space accordingly. Go so far as to indicate what will go in each drawer, closet, shelf, table, etc. If you have trouble envisioning what the room could or should look like, ask a friend or family member to assist you in doing the drawing and planning.

#1
STAY PUT!

When you pick the area in which you are going to work (i.e. the bedroom, kitchen, office), you should make your best effort to collect everything that you will need prior to starting so you do not have to leave the room. Getting up to leave the area in which you are working to retrieve more garbage bags, markers or boxes can be scary because if you leave the room you may never come back. When you start organizing, you'll find things in other rooms that are much more interesting or that need to be tidied up. Before you know it, 20-30 minutes of your two hours is gone, and you've lost track of what you were doing in the original area of work.

While you are organizing, try not to answer the phone, make any calls, check your email, or have anyone around for whom you are responsible. Let people know that you are not available during the time that you are organizing. Distractions will prevent you from reaching your original goal.

So always be prepared to stay confined to the room that you are organizing—at least for the first half of your allotted time while you are sorting (See HALF-TIME Rule in Chapter 7). When you start to put stuff back where it belongs, it's okay to leave the room, but by then you will be on a mission.

A LIST OF WHAT YOU'LL NEED

Create a list of the things that you will need to carry out your plan.

An example list might include:

☆ GARBAGE BAGS (LOTS OF 'EM!)
☆ A file cabinet (for home, too!)
☆ A bigger desk with more storage space
☆ Containers for specific items
☆ Folders for your files and other papers

☆ A lamp
☆ Shelves
☆ A bookcase
☆ Markers for labeling
☆ Boxes to haul away unwanted items
☆ _____
☆ _____
☆ _____
☆ _____

Notice the word "new" was not in front of any of the items above. If you have a lamp, bookcase, desk, etc., that is available, you may be able to recycle it to fit your needs—but don't force it to work. Make sure if you are going to replace a large piece of furniture, such as your desk or file cabinet, that you have a time scheduled to remove the old item so it does not become more clutter!

A REALISTIC TIME SCHEDULE

Time is definitely one of the most miscalculated parts of any plan. You must be realistic when estimating how long you *think* it will take you to accomplish an organizing task.

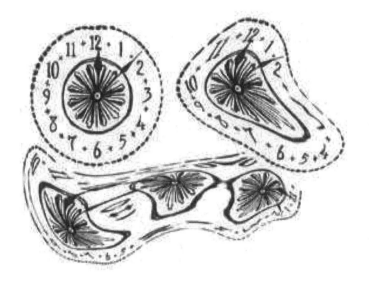

If you think a task will take three hours, in reality, it will probably take about six to get it done in such a way that the long-term effects will take hold. The extra time is needed to deal with those hidden monsters that often rear their ugly heads when you are actually tackling the job. Monsters could include boxes under your desk, laundry baskets full of stuff that are hidden in the back of the closet, the drawer that you thought was empty last week but is full now, etc. In fact, the norm is to double or even triple the amount of time you expect to need. (Sorry, but it's the truth!)

#2

THE HALF-TIME RULE

Just as important as scheduling adequate amounts of time to complete a task is managing that time most effectively.

Here's a scenario with which you are probably familiar. You set out to clean out and organize a room. You have two hours to do it and you mean business. You start out slowly, but then you pick up momentum. Pretty soon, you are on a roll! Things are going places, papers are flying, trashcans are bursting at the seams, and you've created sorting techniques that only you know about.

You are feelin' good. Then you look at the clock. Your two hours are up and you have to go! But wait! How can this be? What was a messy room when you came in to conquer is now a disaster area that resembles the aftermath of a tornado! And you have to leave!

ENTER THE HALF-TIME Rule. Whatever time that you have set aside to organize, spend the first half SORTING and the second half PUTTING AWAY.

Half Time

So if you have two hours, set a timer for one hour. Sort until the timer goes off. Set the timer for one more hour and begin putting things away.

The secret to the success of your plan is to work in an area that is proportionate to the amount of time that you have. If you only have two hours, reorganizing the basement is not likely, but working on the bookshelves is possible. Clearing up your entire office may not be done, but you can purge one file drawer. You get the idea.

Equally important is setting a realistic time limit. Knowing how long you can work before your energy wanes is crucial. If you only have the energy to work for two hours, then stop after two hours. Make sure that you don't overdo it because this will discourage you from future organizing.

Be sure that you keep yourself focused the whole time that you are organizing. It's amazing how much more interesting EVERYTHING else can be—the telephone, the refrigerator, cleaning the house, plucking your eyebrows, getting a tooth pulled, calling your mother-in-law—when you are doing something that you normally put off.

AN URGE TO PURGE

You must be in the mood to throw things away when you begin to take on an organizing project. If you aren't in the mood to get rid of stuff, reschedule for another time. You want to be so excited about throwing things away that you have to warn your kids and pets to stay away from you or they may end up in a trash bag!

As you go through the steps of READY and SET, you should begin to understand why you do the things you do and how you are going to get organized with a plan in spite of what's stopping you from doing so. If you fail to understand either of these steps, you are probably just cramming things into any empty space, and before you know it, the clutter and disorganization will be worse than ever. If you are struggling with creating a plan to get organized, this may be a good time to call in a professional organizer. Visit www.napo.net.

EXERCISE

Create your own sample plan following this example:

ROOM
Basement

DECIDED ACTIVITY FOR ROOM

Watching television
Playing pool
Family gatherings on weekends

SPECIFIC PROBLEMS

1. Basement is a catchall for everything (boxes of old clothes, old stove, broken washing machine, books, old files, magazines, mementos, etc.).
2. I have no time to organize.
3. I don't want to organize.

ACTION PLAN

1. Start in corner by the door.
2. Work on each box or pile, one at a time.
3. Set two hours aside each Saturday.
4. Set a half-hour aside two nights/week.
5. Call the charity for pickup and drop-off instructions.
6. Reward myself—After each session, I get to take a walk for a half-hour.

Which room or area hinders your productivity the most? Once you have chosen a room in which to start, use the following template to create a plan of attack.

ROOM_____

DECIDED ACTIVITY FOR ROOM

_____
_____
_____
_____
_____
_____

SPECIFIC PROBLEMS

_____
_____
_____
_____
_____
_____

ACTION PLAN

_____
_____
_____
_____
_____
_____
_____

REVIEW

TOOLS are the ideas or techniques used to implement organizing systems.

Look around at your space
Ready to get Set

Pattyism #1 Stay Put!
Pattyism #2 The HALF-TIME Rule

YOUR PLAN
➤ A DECIDED ACTIVITY FOR THE ROOM
  Define the purpose of the room.
➤ A LOT O' LOGIC
  Apply logic when arranging space.
➤ A DRAWING
  Make a drawing of the area.
➤ A LIST OF WHAT YOU'LL NEED
  Look at WANT vs. NEED.
➤ A REALISTIC TIME SCHEDULE
  Estimate hours and schedule them.
➤ AN URGE TO PURGE
  Be ready to pitch.
Exercise

_____
_____
_____
_____
_____
_____
_____

So what do you say we move into ACTION?

PART III: GO!

> *"The time for action is now. It's never too late to do something."*
>
> - Carl Sandburg, Author

CHAPTER EIGHT:

GO!

Two things before we <u>GO!</u>

You made it! You have laid the groundwork for successful organizing and I can hear your engine revving...you are so ready to dig into the clutter that you can hardly wait! This is where the fun begins. For the first time in a long time, or maybe ever, you are prepared to successfully organize and OH! what a difference it will make!

Let me preface this chapter with two very important points:

1. In the beginning of Step 3, you will be going through many items that you treasure, love, hate, need, want, must keep, and must throw away. REMEMBER

that you are ONLY sorting at this stage, so there is no need to panic. Everything will stay contained in the area in which you are working and will be touched again—except for the trash—no dumpster diving allowed! If you are not sure of what to do with something, you can simply designate a place or pile for items that you can't categorize just yet. Move on to something else and come back to that pile later on.

2. This is NOT a time to reminisce. When you pick something up, you are to sort it into the right pile, not remember how you acquired it or what you need to do with it. If you stop to reminisce or complete a task, you will waste valuable time. Then you will become discouraged when you see little or no results.

OK, now that that's out of the way, let's GO!

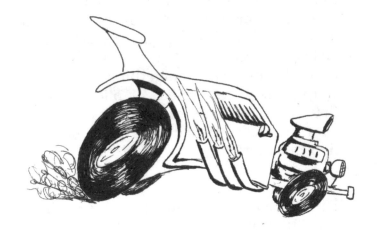

HERE WE GO!

Clutter breaks down into 2 categories:

1. "Stuff" Clutter
2. Paper Clutter

Although the systems that we use to sort
these two types of clutter are different, the
overall process and preparation are the
same. So let's look at the **prep** work needed
for both.

#3
KNOW YOUR PLAN

Before you start, know your plan like the back of your hand. You should have a place to start and a workable timetable. If you have trouble getting started, I recommend that you start small. Choose an area in which you will see quick results. For example, if you are working in the basement and you know that you intend to throw out a stack of newspapers, by all means, bag them up, put them in the recycle bin, and enjoy the newly found space. Just don't be tempted to fill that space up again!

ITEMS NEEDED

First and foremost, you will need a large supply of **garbage bags**. The more bags you have available, the more you will throw away. If you have only one bag, the tendency is to conserve space in that bag for things that "really" need to be tossed. (I should know; I'm a pro at that!)

131

Gather up four or five boxes to contain things as you sort. If you don't have boxes, you can work with laundry baskets, garbage bags, shopping bags, paper bags, large plastic tubs, file boxes, or any container that can hold your sorted stuff for easy mobility later. We will discuss categories and labeling in the next two chapters.

Don't forget to use a timer so that you can implement the critically important HALF-TIME Rule discussed in Chapter 7. Have a few markers, pen and paper, and sticky notes available as well. For paper clutter, you will want to add file folders to the list (hanging <u>and</u> insert folders if you plan to use both). And that's it. Don't invest in anything else yet. It is too soon to know what additional storage containers you may need until you get rid of the clutter. Once you have removed the clutter, you will be better able to decide how to store your remaining items.

#4
THE BUTT RULE

Things that you use daily (especially in an office) should be within easy reach. In other words, you shouldn't have to get up off your butt to get them.

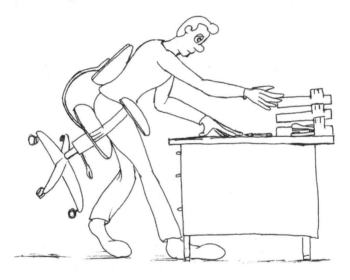

Things that you use less often—weekly or monthly—should be in areas that are easily accessible but require you to get off your butt to get them (a storage closet, across the room).

133

Things that you rarely use should go in the most difficult places to reach (top shelf, off-site storage, basement).

DECISIONS, DECISIONS, DECISIONS

Remember, any type of clutter in your life is nothing more than a big pile of decisions that you have yet to make. The first BIG decision that you have to make is whether you would be happier with or without the clutter in your life.

When you start to organize, you are going to be making a *series* of decisions. You have to be in a decisive frame of mind or you'll never get anywhere. Instead, you'll be pondering what to do with old stuff, moving it from one place to another. BE DECISIVE!

This concludes the prep work, so let's move on to the systems for STUFF and PAPER clutter.

REVIEW

Two things before we GO!
Here we go!
Pattyism #3 – Know your plan
Items needed
Pattyism #4 – The Butt Rule!
Decisions, decisions, decisions

_____
_____
_____
_____
_____
_____
_____
_____
_____
_____
_____
_____
_____
_____
_____
_____
_____
_____
_____
_____
_____
_____
_____
_____
_____

"I hear and I forget. I see and I remember. I do and I understand."

-Confucius, on Learning

CHAPTER NINE:

"Stuff" Clutter

THE "STUFF" CLUTTER SYSTEM

In the GO phase, there are 4 steps for "STUFF":

1. GO through and sort.
2. GO out and deliver.
3. GO home where you belong.
4. GO in the right container.

STEP 1. GO THROUGH AND SORT

With "stuff" clutter, once you start, it's not that difficult to keep going. In fact the hardest part IS starting.

#5
FLASHLIGHT FOCUS

Deciding that you need to organize your whole office or house can be overwhelming. To overcome this feeling of hopelessness, use flashlight focus. Imagine that you are holding a flashlight and shining it on one spot. Concentrate on this spot until it is organized. For example, instead of saying that you are going to organize your whole office, narrow your focus to your desk, and then narrow it further to a drawer. Now it doesn't seem like such a big job. If you want to organize your whole house, start by choosing a room—say your den—then narrow your focus to the bookshelves, and then to the top shelf. Stay focused on that shelf until it is done. Then move on to the next shelf.

Flashlight focus will:

☆ Prevent burnout.
☆ Invite fewer distractions.
☆ Provide results more quickly.
☆ Increase motivation to continue.

As mentioned earlier, you can use boxes, laundry baskets, garbage bags, shopping bags, paper bags, plastic tubs, file boxes, or any container that can hold your sorted stuff for easy mobility later. Designate a container for each different category and label it prominently. If you can't write the category directly on the container, write the category on a piece of paper and attach it to the container. Here are a few suggestions for categories you might use:

☆ TRASH!
☆ Keep
☆ Donate
☆ Sell
☆ Delivery (belongs somewhere else)
☆ Act (or to-do)

Create other categories if you come across something that doesn't fit in any of the above, such as "Gifts to Give," but be sure to dust the item off first before re-gifting! The most important thing is that these categories are meaningful to you so that you can sort easily and without hesitation.

PATTYISM
#6
ODE TO GARBAGE CANS

Garbage cans—think of the garbage cans that you have in your life—at work, at home, outside. Did you ever notice that the smaller the wastebasket, the less you throw away in it? Obviously then, the bigger the receptacle, the more you'll throw away. So I recommend a DUMPSTER! Seriously, be sure to have an appropriately sized can for the task.

Treat your garbage can like a baby...feed it often, keep it in sight, and empty it regularly. If you find your home or office brimming over with papers, perhaps you need to invest in a larger baby...er, wastebasket.

Ask yourself the following questions when you pick something up:

1. Does it still work?
2. Do I really need this?
3. Can I find it somewhere else?
4. When was the last time I used this?
5. Will I die if I don't have this in my life?
6. Would I be happier without this in my life?
7. Who could use this more than I could?
8. Whose birthday is this month (heehee)?

Take one item at a time and put it in the proper container. Is this item something for the trash can or can you donate it to charity? Start by sorting something small, like a drawer or small pile to get warmed up. I recommend starting with something that has been bothering you for quite some time. You will feel so motivated once even a small area of clutter is gone, because you will see that it wasn't so hard after all.

As you SORT, the clutter will spread out into the area in which you are working, so remember to set the timer for the first half of your allotted time to organize. Once the timer goes off, it is time to move on to the next step of PUTTING AWAY. This is critical because if you use up all of your time sorting and have to leave, when you return you will be even more discouraged. The result may be that you will never get the energy to start up again. You may feel like organizing is a lost cause when IT'S NOT!

STEP 2. GO OUT AND DELIVER

When the first HALF of your time is up, stop sorting and deliver the goods to wherever they need to go.

☆ Take out the trash.
☆ Box up or bag the donations and prepare them to be taken to charity (e.g., put them in the car, call charity to pick them up).
☆ Dedicate a spot for items that you may want to sell. Keep them contained in one designated area so they will not get mixed in or confused with other items.
☆ Schedule time for deliveries that need to be made to consignment shops, library, etc.

143

☆ Schedule the Act or To-do items in your calendar (For example, send a thank you for the birthday gift you just found from last year (yikes), fix the broken sweeper, etc.).

As you deliver these items, watch your stuff magically disappear!

STEP 3. GO HOME WHERE YOU BELONG

As part of the second half of your time allotment, put away all of the items that you intend to keep. In doing so, don't just throw them back in a pile or drawer or a closet. Think logically about how you will use items in the future and assign them a home accordingly. This leads us to Step 4.

STEP 4. GO IN THE RIGHT CONTAINER

After you assign a home for your items, some of them may need a container. For example, you may have designated a shelf for photographs but you need photo albums to contain them. Toys might be better in containers that separate toy soldiers from building blocks. Often-used paper forms may need to be separated into mail slots. If you don't have the appropriate container, make a list of what you NEED. Schedule a trip to the store that has the items you need. I urge you to refrain from buying more than you need on impulse, or buying items that you don't need but only want. This will only add to the clutter when you return.

REVIEW

The "stuff" clutter system

There are 4 steps to GO:
>   GO through & sort.
>   GO out & deliver.
>   GO home where you belong.
>   GO in the right container.

Pattyism #5 – Flashlight Focus
Pattyism #6 – Ode to garbage cans

_____
_____
_____
_____
_____
_____
_____
_____
_____
_____
_____
_____
_____
_____
_____
_____
_____
_____
_____
_____

*"Patience, persistence and perspiration make
an unbeatable combination for success."*

- Napolean Hill, author

CHAPTER TEN:

Paper Clutter

ON TO PAPER CLUTTER SYSTEMS...

With papers, decluttering is a little different.
The reason is that there are really only four
things that you can do with a piece of paper,
which is represented by the E.A.S.Y. System.
You start out with four piles labeled:

Eliminate
Act
Send it away
You file it!

Once again, start with an area that will show
results quickly. This could mean a file
drawer, the top of your desk, a pile on the
floor, etc. Wherever you decide to start,
determine the amount of time that you will

147

spend on your organizing session and use the HALF-TIME rule. Set your timer to ring at the halfway point and spend the first half sorting.

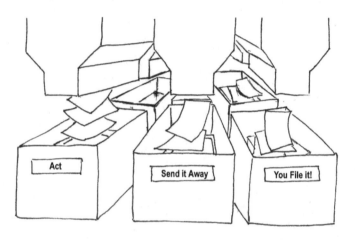

The easiest way to do this is to have a huge trash bag for the papers you ELIMINATE, and put sticky notes labeled ACT, SEND IT AWAY, and FILE on the floor so you have a designated area for each pile. After a while, you may no longer need the notes but they are helpful when you start out. So let's see how this E.A.S.Y. system works!.

ELIMINATE

As you pick up a piece of paper, ask yourself if you need it. If the answer is **NO**, throw it into one of those large garbage bags we talked about earlier.

If the answer is **YES**, you do need it, ask yourself the following questions just to be sure:

1. Can I get it somewhere else? (The Internet, library, a co-worker, emails, computer files, etc.)
2. Is this the only form or location in which the information exists?
3. Would this information be difficult to obtain again?
4. Am I only keeping it because "I might need it someday"?
5. Would I get in trouble if I didn't have this paper?
6. What is the worst possible consequence of not having this piece of paper? If you can live with the results, toss it!
7. Is it recent enough to be useful?
8. Are there any tax or legal implications involved?

<u>A</u>CT

After all of the above questions are answered and you have determined that you need to keep a piece of paper, look at what you need to do with it. If you have to keep something because you need to do something with it, it would go in the ACT pile. This could include a bill that needs to be paid, an invoice that needs to be researched, a proposal that needs to be reviewed or written, a letter from a client with whom you need to follow up, a notice for a meeting you need to attend, an R.S.V.P. for a networking event, etc.

You may be inclined to DO the items as you come across them, especially if they are quick items. Now is NOT the time to do them. You have to keep in mind that this precious time has been allotted to organizing. Rest assured, you will touch each Action item again in the second half of your allotted time. That is when you will decide WHEN to ACT on them.

SEND IT AWAY

If you must keep something but it doesn't belong to you, it should go in the pile labeled SEND IT AWAY. Notice I said put it in a pile. Do not deliver it to the person or place where it belongs because you will never come back. Instead, write the name of the person to whom it belongs or its destination directly on the item or on a sticky note and attach it to the paper. Later, when you go to deliver it, you won't have to think about where it should go. You'll want to put that pile by the door since it will be leaving soon.

<u>Y</u>OU FILE IT!

And last but certainly not least, if you pick up a piece of paper that you NEED to keep but which doesn't require action, then you should put it in the FILE pile. This pile would include items that need to go into an existing file or need to have a new file made.

That's it! You do this sorting until the alarm tells you that you have reached HALF-TIME. At first, the sorting process will seem to go a little slowly, but the decision-making gets easier and easier. You will let go of more things as you progress because you become more aware of the reasons for NOT keeping them.

I'VE SORTED—NOW WHAT?

For the second half of your allotted time, start by taking out the TRASH. Next, pick up the SEND IT AWAY items and deliver them. If they need to be put in a different room or office, take them there now. If you need to take them home or to work, put them in the car. When you return, you should see serious results: the place that you just cleared is empty (please leave it that way!), the trash is gone, and the SEND IT AWAY pile is gone. Quite motivating! All that's left to deal with are the ACT pile and the FILE pile.

Let's start with the ACT pile. There are two things that you can do with these action items.

1. SCHEDULE THEM!

You can and should schedule time in your day planner to do the items that need to be "acted" on. This does not mean simply adding the items to your to-do list. It is too easy to overlook tasks on your to-do list because they aren't necessarily things that you want to do. Instead, assign each task a particular time slot on a specific day. This is a magnificent way to remember to do things. Plus, by scheduling a specific time, you will be more likely to accomplish the task.

2. USE A PaperConnect™ TICKLER FILE

Scheduling an ACT item is helpful, but it doesn't solve the problem of what to do with the papers involved with the ACT item. If you've never heard of or used a tickler file system before, you are in for a simple treat.

The PaperConnect™ TICKLER FILE is a set of 44 hanging file folders with an insert folder inside of each one. They are labeled Needs Information, 1-31 for the days of the month, and January – December for the months of the year. To use the tickler file, simply DECIDE what day you are going to act on a piece of paper, and put it in the folder that corresponds to that date or month. That's it! It is designed to "tickle" your memory when something is due.

If you are not going to act on something this month, place it in the appropriately labeled monthly folder. At the beginning of each month, pull all papers out of the current month's folder. Decide which day during that month that you will complete each task, and put the corresponding paper into one of the 1-31 folders corresponding to that date.

Keep the tickler file in a desk drawer, a rolling cart, a crate, or anywhere close by. You must **CHECK IT DAILY!** Otherwise, it's not worth a nickel.

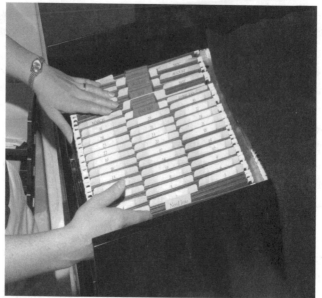

Photo by © Connie Karaffa

The tickler file is great for work, home and home offices! The "Needs Info" file is ideal for holding papers while you wait for a return call or more information from someone else. This keeps them off of your desk but in a safe place for quick retrieval when you need them. A tickler file can be used for the following purposes and many more!

- ☆ Paying your bills
- ☆ Client follow-up
- ☆ Travel information
- ☆ Conference information

- ☆ Quarterly taxes
- ☆ Renewals
- ☆ Birthday cards
- ☆ Important events
- ☆ RSVP's
- ☆ Anything date sensitive!

It will:

- ☆ Keep your desk cleared off.
- ☆ Save you time looking for papers.
- ☆ Cure "If you can't see it, you forget it".

It's so simple and easy to use; you'll wonder how you ever lived without it!

THE LAST PILE—THE FILE PILE!

NOTE: As you make files, keep in mind that 80% of what you keep in your files, you will never touch again. So before you put papers into folders, be sure that you NEED to keep them.

This last pile will be the most time consuming to deal with. As a Professional Organizer, it is my belief that every person should have a filing system designed around how he or she thinks. Since I am not with you to personally run through the 3-step system of READY, SET, and GO, you will have to do the analysis by getting to know your beliefs, behaviors, habits, and style.

Since everyone thinks differently, some of the suggestions in this book may not suit your personal needs. That's the beauty of getting to know yourself and learning to overcome your own limitations. You can find out what would and would not work for you based on this information.

#7
NO TWO ARE ALIKE

I have to emphasize one thing...each person that I work with is different. I thrive on getting to know how each individual functions, thinks, works, and makes decisions. Therefore, I have to customize the process and systems that are used. Here's an illustration of this:

If I was in a room with 15 people and I asked the question, "How do you file your cable television bill?" The answers vary from:

☆ Under A for AT&T (or company name)
☆ Under B for Bills
☆ Under C for Cable
☆ Under P for Paid bills
☆ Under T for Television
☆ Under U for Utilities
☆ I pay online; I don't receive a cable bill
☆ In a chronological accordion file
☆ In a big folder with all my bills
☆ I throw it away after I pay it (good answer!)

There are almost as many responses as people. This is what I mean when I say you have to design your filing system around how YOU think. Where is your cable bill filed?

FILING SYSTEMS

Depending on how you think, your filing system may reflect one of the following simple systems or perhaps another not listed here:

☆ Alphabetical
☆ Numerical
☆ Category or Subject

☆ Geographical
☆ Color-coded
☆ A combination of these

ALPHABETICAL

If you took all of your files and put them in alphabetical order, you would have an easy system to use. An alphabetical system works best when you don't have hundreds and hundreds of files. If you do have too many files, it becomes cumbersome and you may become overwhelmed trying to remember if your gasoline receipts are filed under F for Fuel, A for Automobile, or C for Car! This may become an excuse to fall back into disorganization. If locating documents becomes difficult, a file index may be helpful (See Chapter 12).

There are no exact guidelines on when to use an alphabetical system, but if you have more than fifty files, you may want to consider breaking your files down into **categories** (see CATEGORY below).

NUMERICAL

Numerical systems tend to be used in places such as doctors' offices, where they use a birth date or a social security number to locate a file. Car dealerships use numerical systems as well, filing records using the last 4 or 5 digits of the Vehicle ID number. If your files can be organized by using a consistent number on every folder, this system may work for you.

CATEGORY

There are no one-size-fits-all filing systems, but roughly 85% of the time, my clients are best suited to using some variation of the Category System. I believe that this is true because most people naturally think in categories.

Start by sorting the FILE pile into piles of related items. To speed up the process, write the category of each pile on a sticky note or piece of paper and place it in front of each pile. This takes the guesswork out of sorting.

Another way to design a category-based system is to create an organizational flow chart before you sort (see below). If you are a visual person, this tool might help you to see the big picture before you begin.

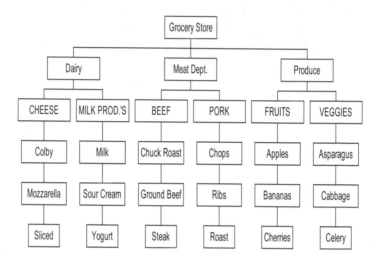

Organizational Flow Chart

To make the chart, draw a square at the top of a piece of paper. That square represents the main category. Next, draw a box underneath the main category for each sub-category and label each accordingly. Then underneath each subcategory, draw boxes to represent the files that fall into that category. The grocery store example above demonstrates how this works.

Once you have determined your categories, you can alphabetize within each one. If you want to go another step, it is helpful to color-code by category as well. With the above grocery store example, you might put Veggies into green folders, Cheeses into yellow folders, and fruits into red folders. For your own files, you might put financial files into green folders, medical files into red folders, and administrative forms into blue folders.

Whenever possible, choose colors that relate in some way to the folder's contents. As you work with your filing system, you will be able to immediately identify what category the folder's contents falls into just by the color. This will help speed up your filing.

Of course, all of your files are not in your FILE pile. You may have file cabinets full of files that need to be sorted and categorized. In order to incorporate all of your files into the category system, you need to pull each file out and sort it into the categories that you have created. For an easier way to do this, see Working Backwards in Chapter 12.

PATTYISM
#8
MASTER PILER
TO MASTER FILER

Some people rank as Master Pilers. These are folks that can stack papers on their desks, floor, chairs, credenza, or any flat (and sometimes not so flat) surface. I've been fortunate enough to see papers stacked on printers, keyboards, calculators, phones, and an unbelievable assortment of other items.

I am always impressed by the sophistication of the architecture of the pile; papers zig and zag to give the pile the stability it needs to withstand even more height. If you are one of the Master Pilers of the world, while I appreciate your piling skills, I encourage you to disassemble your artful structures one at a time. Convert your master piles into master files!

GEOGRAPHICAL

If you work with areas, regions, multiple locations, or territories, a geographical filing system is ideal. Sort your files into distinct geographical areas. This may include regions, territories, districts, etc. Within each area, you may want to alphabetize and/or color-code the folders.

:	:
:	:
:	:
E	5
D	4
C	3
B	2
A	1
ALPHABETICAL	**NUMERICAL**

:	:
:	:
:	:
:	NETWORKING
WEST	MARKETING
EAST	FINANCES
SOUTH	BILLS
NORTH	ADMINISTRATIVE
GEOGRAPHICAL	**CATEGORY**

COLOR-CODED

As mentioned above in the category and geographical filing systems, consider assigning a color to a specific subject or area. What happens if you have more subjects or areas than colors of folders? To further distinguish one from another, you could:

☆ Use color-coded labels
☆ Use colored plastic tabs
☆ Use colored markers to write on the label
☆ Use colored or fun-shaped stickers
☆ Use only left, middle or right tabbed insert folders with specific colors.

For example, if you had different subjects in red folders, you could use green labels on one and blue on the other to differentiate them.

CAUTION: If you choose to color-code your filing system, be sure to have enough of each color on hand. If you run out of one color, the tendency is to pick up a folder of another color, which will completely nullify the effectiveness of the color-coded system. Alternatively, you may decide to set the paper aside in a pile, and before you know it, the pile will get bigger and bigger, and you're back to being a Master Piler. Therefore, it is important for you to always have plenty of supplies in stock.

COMBINATION OF THE ABOVE SYSTEMS

As seen in the above examples, combining systems can be very effective. Be creative and try to find a system that works for you. If you listen to yourself, you will probably know right away what will and will not work for you. If you can find the file you need in a minute or less, then your system is effective. If you can't find a file when you need it, then you know your system is not effective and you need to review the types of systems on the previous pages and choose another that would be better suited to your style.

PATTYISM

#9
WHERE DO I PUT IT?

When you are deciding where to put something, especially papers, the question you should ask yourself is NOT "where do I put it" BUT "where will I find it?"

Think about that for a minute. You can put something anywhere, but is that where you will look for it when you need it? This is especially important when you are deciding how to label a file. Don't get sloppy by just marking the label with the first thing that comes to your mind. THINK about the future. When you go to retrieve this file, where will you go to look for it?

Getting organized is one thing, but how do you stay that way? Part IV offers more tools, ideas, and tips that are sure to keep you on the road to organizational bliss.

REVIEW

Pattyism #7 No two are alike
Pattyism #8 Master Piler to Master Filer
Pattyism #9 Where do I put it?

PAPER CLUTTER SYSTEM
☆ **E**liminate
☆ **A**ct
☆ **S**end it away
☆ **Y**ou file it!

I've sorted...now what?
Schedule them!
PaperConnect ™ Tickler File

FILING SYSTEMS

☆ Alphabetical
☆ Numerical
☆ Category
☆ Geographical
☆ Color-coded
☆ A combination of these

_____
_____
_____
_____
_____
_____
_____
_____

PART IV: MAINTENANCE

"Motivation will almost always beat mere talent."

- Norman R. Augustine

CHAPTER ELEVEN:

"Stuff" Maintenance

You are now armed with the tools that will help you declutter your life. If you use these tools to reach your organizational goal, what is the trick to living a life without clutter for more than ten minutes? Simple: keep the Circle of Change that includes belief, behavior, and tools very tight. With the tools that you now have to get organized, the challenge is to change your beliefs and behavior permanently. Inspired by your desire to get organized, you must develop new habits over a period of time until they become natural. It may not be easy, but with consistency and a positive mental attitude, your new good habits can replace your old bad habits.

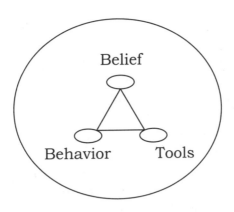

THE CIRCLE OF CHANGE

We know that clutter breaks down into two types: stuff clutter and paper clutter. Let's look at each separately again.

KEEPING THE "STUFF" AWAY

After you have made all of those painful decisions on what to keep, sell, donate, and throw away, how do you keep from replenishing the stock?

NEED VS. WANT

If you really want to keep the order that you have now achieved, you MUST change your behavior and beliefs. If you believe that you need to have more things, you must decide what you will dispose of to make room for each new item, or else you will recreate a cluttered environment. Better yet, start to question WHY you must buy an item *before* you buy it. Are you succumbing to advertising? Can you live without it? Do you *really* want to spend your hard-earned money on it? If you change your beliefs of need vs. want, you will see changes begin to occur in your life.

THE ENEMY

In Chapter 3, **shopping** was referred to as the great enemy of the disorganized. If you have too much stuff, you need to watch your "intake." If you are shopping and you do decide to bring a new item into your life, you must decide then and there what item you will be discarding, donating, selling, or giving to a friend.

For example, after lots of hard work, Bradley finally has the use of his garage for the first time in 14 years. He is able to park his truck in there now, something he thought would *never* happen. Then one day, Bradley goes to the hardware store and he sees a workbench that he'd give his right arm to have. Some habits are hard to break. At that moment, instead of impulsively purchasing the workbench, Bradley must ask himself:

☆ Do I NEED or WANT this new workbench?
☆ If I NEED it, where will I put it?
☆ If I do buy it, what will I be getting rid of?

Empty Space

DOES NOT EQUAL

Available Space!

Empty space does not equal available space. You have to continually challenge your belief system. If Bradley believes that the empty garage equals available space for storing stuff, it will become just that and he'll buy the workbench. If he believes, however, that a garage is meant to house his truck, he will likely stick to that belief and adjust his behavior accordingly. This means that Bradley would not allow the new workbench to crowd out his truck.

In order to maintain the decluttered environment that you have just worked so hard to attain, you must question your actions. This is healthy because it helps you to realize that not everything you do is set in stone. You can dispel some of the myths that you've held since birth and choose your own values to replace them.

ONE IN – ONE OUT

Kathy goes to the store and sees a pair of pants that she MUST have. Kathy needs to go through the same series of questions:

1. Do I NEED or WANT these pants?
2. If I NEED them, where will I put them (do I have room)?
3. If I do buy them, what will I be getting rid of?

If Kathy NEEDS new pants, then she should buy them. Now she must decide what she will be removing from her closet before she buys the pants. The key is to follow through with the disposal of the other item. If Kathy WANTS the new pants but doesn't NEED them, she must ask herself if she can wait a week and walk away. If she even remembers next week that they were on her radar screen the week before, Kathy needs to ask questions 2 & 3 above again, decide what will be leaving her closet to make room for the new pants, and stick to her decision.

In order to make really quick progress in decluttering your life, instead of getting rid of one item to make room for the new, get rid of two or three or four! So you can use the One in—one out rule, One in—two out rule, One in—three out rule, and so on. Obviously the higher the OUT number, the faster you will see results.

ONE OUT – ONE IN

If you have ever experienced the phenomenon that clothes shrink when you put them in a closet (who knew?), try what I do. I work in reverse; I use the One OUT – one IN rule. I clean my closets out twice a year, in the spring and the fall as I change seasonal clothes (OUT). I then determine what is missing from my wardrobe—I need a new white blouse, for instance—and then I go shopping to fill those gaps (IN).

If I happen to be at the mall and I see something that I just love and want and it is on sale, I make a mental note of what I can donate to make room for the new item. We have small closets in our home (by design) so I know that space is limited. This not only prevents me from having more stuff than I NEED, it also helps me to save money.

The One in—one out and the One OUT – one IN rule can apply to anything that you bring into your life, not just clothes. It can work for furniture, linens, food, shoes, books, computer equipment, or office supplies: you name it.

Parents, this is a fabulous rule to teach your children. What a great gift to give to your children by teaching them to be generous and organized at the same time.

There has to be room for the new items that you bring into your life. Buying things just because you want them is no longer going to work because you will end up right back where you started.

When you finally get out from under the clutter, you will probably never want to go back to that way of life again. Therefore it is imperative that you change your beliefs and behavior while using the tools to be organized.

P.S. If you have lots of clutter and you can't pass up a garage sale, you may want to reconsider this hobby. You are simply bringing someone else's discards home and cluttering your life. AVOID GARAGE SALES AT ALL POSSIBLE COST (unless it's your own)!

REVIEW

KEEPING THE "STUFF" CLUTTER AWAY

Need VS. Want

☆ Do I NEED or WANT this?
☆ If I NEED it, where will I put (do I have room)?
☆ If I do buy it, what will I be getting rid of?

THE ENEMY = Shopping
One in – One out
One out – one in
Empty space does not equal available space!

_____
_____
_____
_____
_____
_____
_____
_____
_____
_____
_____
_____
_____
_____
_____
_____
_____
_____

*"Good habits are as addictive as bad habits,
and a lot more rewarding."*

- Harvey Mackay, businessman and author

CHAPTER TWELVE:

Paper Maintenance

PAPER CLUTTER - STOP THE MADNESS!

So your home or work office is now organized and your papers are neatly filed. You used the E.A.S.Y. system for sorting and have designed a filing system for those papers. But don't look now, here comes the mailman!

INCOMING!

Now you have to ask the $64,000 question: how do you control the continuous daily flood of papers that enters your life? It helps that you have a system for handling your existing papers, but how do you process and keep a handle on the daily onslaught of new papers?

179

THE MAIL

Through rain, sleet, hail, or snow...you know the saying. That mail is going to show up whether you like it or not. So how can you best handle the daily mail?

1. ALWAYS open your mail daily, with a letter opener, over a wastebasket. By doing so, you can get rid of junk mail **before** it has a chance to form a pile on your desk or work area. Not only that, you can eliminate half the volume of what

remains just by discarding the envelopes that the mail came in.

2. Open your mail in the same spot EVERY day. Don't change your routine. This designated spot should include:

☆ A large wastebasket
☆ A PaperConnect™ Tickler File
☆ A calendar
☆ A letter opener

As you open something, ask yourself right then and there when you are going to (really) act on this item. Look at your calendar and see when you have the time to do it. Place that item in the corresponding folder of the Tickler File. This prevents the mail from piling up. Make the decision as you hold the mail in your hand. Don't postpone the decision and end up facing HUGE piles of mail at a later date.

3. To receive less commercial advertising mail, you can register for the DMA's Mail Preference Service (MPS), which allows you to "opt out" of national mailings. For more information, visit them on the web at www.the-dma.org. This will reduce the volume of junk mail considerably...from a flood to a trickle!

4. Check with your creditors to see if they offer e-invoicing. Instead of receiving a hard copy of your bill, you receive an email invoice that you can view and pay over a secure line. Each company that offers this has their own set of guidelines, so check with each one. Along these same lines, you may want to look into online banking to save time and reduce the hassle of writing checks and sealing envelopes!

OTHER INCOMING PAPERS

Mail is not the only culprit that adds to the piles of paper. All day long, your inbox is filling up. People hand you papers on the run. Family members pawn their pulpy masses on you every chance they get. Interoffice mail arrives three times a day. You are the lucky recipient of 3 daily newspapers, 4 weekly newsletters, 5 monthly journals, and schoolwork for 3 children. You are being bombarded all the time with new paper clutter that needs immediate attention. What are you to do?

1. Similar to handling the mail, you must decide how to handle these papers as soon as they arrive. WHEN are you going to ACT on those papers? Does each paper need action by you, or can you delegate it? Can you throw it away? Always have your PaperConnect™ Tickler File near you, along with a calendar. If you put the papers down, they are likely to be buried under tomorrow's incoming papers and forgotten.

   REMEMBER: The PaperConnect™ Tickler File is a "home" for the papers that need action. The tickler file works best if you take the time to schedule your action items into a time slot in your daily planner as well as placing them in the tickler file. Not only will you be more likely to complete the task if you have scheduled it in your planner, but you will also have a cross-reference for your tickler file in your planner notes. Don't forget: YOU MUST CHECK THE TICKLER FILE DAILY!

2. If you are a "Master Piler," forming new habits to deal with papers may take time. You have the tools and a new filing system that reflects how YOU think. Now you must change your beliefs and behaviors to a mindset congruent with

continuing these new habits. Before you put a piece of paper on an existing pile or (heaven forbid) start a whole new pile, STOP. Invest the 30 seconds to put it away NOW. Later on, when you have a clear work area, you'll be glad that you did

3. Be realistic about your reading materials and realize that you can't read it all. You can't and don't have to know everything that happens in the world. Believe me, if something big happens, you'll know it. It is easy to underestimate how much time it really takes to read every newspaper, magazine, and newsletter you receive. It is impossible to have a full life and tackle a 3-month backlog of reading material along with the current stack. If you are always backed up in your reading, let some of your subscriptions go or donate them to a senior center or doctor's office. Bet you won't even miss them!

4. Resist the urge to make extra copies "just in case." Don't print documents from your computer that you can read on the screen. The less paper you start with, the easier it will be to manage.

BONUS MAINTENANCE IDEAS!

INDEX IT!

Not all incoming items that enter your life need action. Many times they just need to be filed. Therefore, no matter how many files you have, you need to have an index to help you retrieve and replace them. An index is nothing more than a list of what is in each file drawer or location.

1. To make a simple index, try this method. Label all of your drawers with numbers (or letters if you prefer), starting with number 1 as in the illustration below. If you have desk drawers, credenza drawers, or any location that houses files, include and label them as well.

2. Get a tablet and write DRAWER 1 and then list each and every file in that drawer. Proceed with DRAWER 2,3,4,5, and so on.

3. For best searching results, consider creating your index in a spreadsheet (Microsoft Excel®, Lotus®, etc.), database (Microsoft Access ®) or a document that is

searchable by keyword. (See sample below.)

An index not only helps you retrieve your files easily; it also helps you determine where you should file a document before you approach the drawer. An added bonus is that when you are away from your files, others can use your index to find information; they can determine where to find what they need in your absence without calling you. If you are concerned about privacy, make public only those files that you feel are appropriate.

INDEX EXAMPLE OF FILE DRAWERS

DRAWER 1

		□AD-Visa Acct
		□AD-Taxes
		□AD-Receipts
	□**AD-Phones**	
	□**AD-Legal**	
	□**AD-Internet**	
□ **AD-Goals**		
🗁Savings		
🗁Checking		
□**AD-Bank**		
□**AD-Auto**		
	ADMINISTRATION	

DRAWER 2

		🗁Past Ads
		🗁Future ideas
		□**MKG-Yellow Pages**
	🗁Pricing	
	🗁Availability	
	□**MKG-Conf. Rooms**	
🗁Radio		
🗁Newspaper		
🗁Ads - New		
□**MKG-Ads**		
	MARKETING	

□   Bold Font = Hanging Folders
🗁   Regular Font = Insert (Manila) Folders inside

The **index** below is based on the above file drawers. The color of the folder is listed for easy and quick reference. Items such as Checking and Savings are indented to show that they are separate manila folders within the hanging folder labeled Bank.

FILE INDEX

DRAWER 1 - ADMINISTRATION - AD - Blue
Auto
Bank
Checking
Savings
Goals
Internet
Legal
Phones
Receipts
Taxes
Visa

DRAWER 2 - MARKETING - MKG - Purple
Ads
Ads – New
Newspaper
Radio
Conference Rooms
Availability
Pricing
Yellow Pages
Future Ideas
Past Ads

The abbreviation next to the color is an *identifier* that is written on the label of each folder within a given category. For example, the first folder – Auto – would be in a blue folder labeled AD—Auto. This lets you know that Auto falls under the Administration category. This is helpful if you use color-coding and you have more than one category per color. You may see two blue folders on your desk, but the identifier differentiates the category quickly.

WORKING BACKWARDS

Usually, an index is made up **after** you have your new filing system in place. However, an index can be a good way to **start** organizing for some people. The first step is to label your drawers starting with 1. Next, go into each drawer and list the contents on paper. Now, rather than sorting through file drawers to see what you have, you can scan your newly created index and determine what you have, what you can get rid of, which items are in the same category that can be filed together, what needs to be archived, etc. An index gives you an overview of everything that you have, and sometimes having that "big picture" can be helpful. Plus, it may be a little less overwhelming to look at a paper list than

staring at all of those files! If you enter the index into a spreadsheet, you can work from that easily without having to rewrite the contents. However you choose to create your index, you must make a commitment to keeping it updated in order to maintain your newly-organized state.

KEEPING TABS

If you use plastic tabs on your hanging file folders to label the contents, you probably do what most people do; you start labeling on the left tab, middle tab, right tab, left tab, middle tab, right tab, and so on. Then when you add a new file, the whole system is wrecked! Each time you add a new file, you either have to go back and replace all of the tabs or put up with the tabs that are all jumbled up!

To keep your file tabs looking neat, try this method. Anything that starts with:

A-G—put on the left tab

H-P—put on the middle tab

Q-Z—put on the right tab

This works with alphabetical, category, and geographical filing systems.

TAB BREAKDOWN

		_ Z _
		_ Y _
		_ X _
		_ W _
		_ V _
		_ U _
		_ T _
		_ S _
		_ R _
		_ Q _
	- P -	
	- O -	
	- N -	
	- M -	
	- L -	
	- K -	
	- J -	
	- I -	
	- H -	
_ G _		
_ F _		
_ E _		
_ D _		
_ C _		
_ B _		
_ A _		

Patty Kreamer

Be creative! If your files break down with A-F in one drawer, you can break it into 3 with:

A-B—on the left tab
C-D—on the middle tab
E-F—on the right tab

If you want to use all five tab placements of the hanging file folder, break it down with:

A-E—on the left tab
F-J—on the second tab
K-O—on the middle tab
P-T—on the fourth tab
U-Z—on the right tab

If you use numerical systems, simply break down the numbers into three or five sections per drawer.

0-3—on the left tab
4-6—on the middle tab
7-9—on the right tab

OR

0-1—on the left tab
2-3—on the second tab
4-5—on the middle tab
6-7—on the fourth tab
8-9—on the right tab

No matter how you choose to break down your files, this system will allow a new file to fall right into place. The best part is that retrieval is even simpler because you can ignore most of the drawer and focus on a smaller section.

Another suggestion regarding plastic tabs— place the plastic tab on the front of the hanging folder rather than on the back. This way, the contents of the hanging folder won't hide the tab. Also, when you spot the tab that you need, just grab it and pull it towards you to open the file. Try it!

Even if you don't use plastic tabs, you can arrange manila folders using the tab system described above. Just be sure that you have enough of each tab position on hand at all times. Spending an extra 5 seconds to think about which tab position you need will be worthwhile when you retrieve your file later. Have extras of each tab position handy in a nearby spot.

MAKING A FILE —WHAT A DRAG!

One of the biggest drawbacks of making a new file can be gathering the supplies. They never seem to be within reach. When all the supplies you need are not readily available, that is when you start to form piles. By taking a little time to plan, you can make your life easier by trying this idea:

1. If you are using hanging file folders, take one or two boxes of them—or if you are using multiple colors, take 5-10 folders of each color—and hang them in a drawer that has enough space to house 25-50 hanging folders. If you have no such drawer, consider using a milk crate or file box with rails that can hold hanging file folders.

2. Place a manila (insert) folder inside of each hanging folder. Make sure if you are using color-coded files that you match the interior folder with the hanging file folders.

3. Drop a plastic tab inside of the manila folder. Be sure, again, that it is the right color. This will ultimately be placed on the hanging folder.

4. Drop a white paper tab inside of the manila folder as well. This is the little perforated tab that comes with the box of hanging folders that you write or place your label on.

5. If you use labels or a particular marker or pen for consistency, put them in the very first folder. Be sure to return them to their home after each use.

Ta-da! You now have 25-50 filing sets. If you need to make a new file, everything you need is readily at hand. Just grab the first folder and you are on your way. The secret is to spend less time hunting and more time producing.

Before I leave a client's office, I normally prepare 1-2 boxes of files for them for future use. They will be more likely to maintain their filing systems if there are no obstacles (like misplaced supplies) holding them back.

As you may have guessed by now, I like to work backwards. So try this. BEFORE you start to organize your papers, especially if you are organizing alone, spend five minutes preparing these folders and filing supplies to save yourself time and energy as you are building your new system.

GENERAL MAINTENANCE IDEAS

Maintenance is not difficult if you make it a priority by building it into your everyday routine. To keep your files in shape, I recommend the following tips:

1. Stop using your files as a catchall for every paper that comes in. Remember that 80% of what you file away will never be touched or looked at again. Make a decision about what to do with that paper the FIRST time you touch it.

2. Purge your papers regularly. I recommend twice a year, perhaps at year-end or just after New Years, and again in June or July. If you have a regular slow time each year, use that time for purging. On a daily basis, you can purge files every time you retrieve them.

3. Schedule a time at the end of each day to clean up your work area. If done each day, it should only require 10-20 minutes. This time should include putting things away and preparing your paperwork for the next day. Without tons of paperwork to climb over each morning, you will be able to start each day more refreshed and focused. You will find yourself being more productive as well!

REVIEW

Paper Clutter—Stop the Madness!
Incoming!
The Mail
Other incoming papers
Bonus maintenance ideas!
Index it!
Working backwards
Keeping tabs
Making a file – what a drag!
General maintenance ideas

_____
_____
_____
_____
_____
_____
_____
_____
_____
_____
_____
_____
_____
_____
_____
_____

*"I'd rather be a failure at something I love
than a success at something I hate."*

- George Burns

CHAPTER THIRTEEN:
Put a Bow on it!

Let's wrap this up and put a bow on it!
Below is a short review followed by two real
life stories of clients who have tried the
processes in this book.

READY, SET, GO!

☆ **READY...**Get to know yourself and why you do the things that you do. Question your beliefs and behaviors.

☆ **SET...**Take a look around at the area in which you will work, set up a plan complete with time schedule, and identify the tools you will need to get organized.

☆ **GO!...**Put your plan into action and see results as you GO!

REVIEW

Pattyism #1 - Stay Put!
Always be prepared to stay confined to the room you are organizing—at least for the first half of your allotted time as you sort.

Pattyism #2 - Half-Time Rule
Whatever time that you have set aside to organize, spend the first half SORTING and the second half PUTTING AWAY.

Pattyism #3 – Know your plan
Before you start, know your plan like the back of your hand. I recommend that you start small—choose an area in which you will see quick results.

Pattyism #4 – The Butt Rule!
Things you use daily should be within easy reach. Things you use less often should be further away, but accessible. Things you rarely use should go in the least convenient storage spaces.

Pattyism #5 – Flashlight Focus
Imagine that you are holding a flashlight and shining it on one spot. Concentrate on this spot until it is organized.

Pattyism #6 – Ode to garbage cans
Be sure to have an appropriately sized can for the task. Treat your garbage can like a baby...feed it often, keep it in sight, and empty it regularly.

Pattyism #7 – No two are alike
You have to design your filing system around how YOU think. Be yourself, and do what works for you!

Pattyism #8 – Master Piler to Master Filer

Convert your master piles into master files!

Pattyism #9 – Where do I put it?

When you are deciding where to put something, especially papers, the question you should ask yourself is NOT "where do I put it" BUT "where will I find it?"

REAL LIFE STORIES

Does Ready, Set, GO! work in the real world? Read on as two of my clients share how the processes in this book have helped them to get where they needed to be.

JoAnn McBride
Lawrence County Tourist Promotion Agency

What made you want to get organized before we met? Was there a final straw?

When we moved into our new office three years ago, we were unable to bring the filing cabinets we used with us; therefore, in order to get up and running, we just "plopped" the files everywhere. It took us forever to find a file. We also found that there was not a coordinated place for the files. Everyone took a file to her desk, so if someone was gone for the day, we had no clue where the file was.

How many times have you attempted getting organized on your own? What worked and didn't work?

Our organization didn't really make sense. The only thing that worked is that we asked each other all the time where the file was. This is okay in a small two-person office such as ours, but it wasn't efficient and it was a definite time-waster.

As we worked together, did you see a pattern or process that you have been able to repeat on your own?

We actually used Patty's guidelines extensively. My assistant and I discussed what categories we needed for the different file drawers and then agreed upon which files should be placed in those drawers. Using an integrated color-coded system, we labeled the files and file drawers. We even took the process one step further by using color-coded computer disks that match the various filing categories.

Since getting organized, what changes can you see (if any) in your habits, stress level, and overall production?

The PaperConnect™ Tickler File has given me an uncluttered desk and mind. It's amazing how it helped not only in the office, but also in my own personal habits.

In regard to the office: when the mail comes in, I immediately sort it and place it in a date in the tickler file. For instance if there is a meeting I plan to attend on the 15th, I respond to the invitation immediately, note on the invitation that I responded, write it on my calendar and file the invitation for one day prior to the meeting. That gives me all the reminders I need for that particular meeting. Prior to leaving at night, I organize my tasks for the next day. That way when I sit down at my desk in the morning, I don't feel overwhelmed. Each morning I pull out the tasks placed in the tickler file from the previous day.

In regard to my personal habits: When I pay bills at home, I try and pay them all at once but not mail them until a few days before each particular bill is due. I place the bill in the tickler file on the date I want to mail it. Lately, when I see a greeting card that I think will be suitable for a friend or family member, I purchase it immediately and place it in the tickler file for the month I want to send it.

In getting organized, what was the biggest obstacle that you had to overcome?

As the director of the agency and the employee with the most seniority, it fell to me to do the cleaning of the old files because the others didn't know what was or wasn't important. It took us a long time. We started in the winter but had to curtail the process over the busy summer season. We didn't start again until things slowed down in late fall. Everything takes times but this was worth the wait!

Kevin Lamb
Director of Planning,
Carnegie Mellon University

What made you want to get organized before we met? Was there a final straw?

There were piles of papers and folders throughout our office suite and especially in my office! I felt like the walls were closing in on me. We spent way too much time looking for things and often not finding what we went looking for. And, it all looked so sloppy and unprofessional. It was demoralizing.

How many times have you attempted getting organized on your own? What worked and didn't work?

Quite a few times, with varying levels of success. Annual clean up day has been effective...every year we have a clean out day and we get rid of barrels full of papers, folders, books and obsolete equipment.

As we worked together, did you see a pattern or process that you have been able to repeat on your own?

Yes. It may sound terribly basic, but I learned how to take a pile of papers and folders and work through them at a pretty good pace, deciding what to pitch, what to keep and where to keep it, and what to send to others. This was combined with the basic task of keeping a directory (index) of files on my computer desktop, which serves as a ready reference.

Since getting organized, what changes can you see (if any) in your habits, stress level, and overall production?

I see subtle but important changes. First, our office is no longer demoralizing! Second, I throw away far more than I ever did before (not proud of the waste, but very proud of not having clutter all over the office.) And, third, I am definitely less stressed and much more focused on the substance of my work. I actually use the files more often and much more effectively than when the drawers were bulging so badly that I found them a big waste of time and rarely bothered to use them.

In getting organized, what was the biggest obstacle that you had to overcome?

Because ours was a group effort, the biggest challenge was getting all seven people in our office to take the effort seriously. When they did come around, it was an awesome experience!

YOU ARE READY & SET...NOW GO!

As you have just read from JoAnn and Kevin, getting organized is possible! Now that you have heard how others have succeeded by putting forth their effort, time, and energy, IT'S YOUR TURN!

You have what it takes; now take the time to do it. Don't pressure yourself to get organized all at once or you will be discouraged. Take small steps and work toward your end goal. But get started, or you'll never get there! Once you declutter your life, both physically and mentally, you will be so glad that you did! You will finally have time for YOU, while enjoying a happy and stress-free life.

If you feel that you still need some additional help, please consider hiring a professional organizer to get you started on the right path.

I am interested in your success story, so please email it to me through my website at www.ByeByeClutter.com.   I would love to hear from you!   Feel free to email me with any questions that you may have as well.

I wish you the best of luck!

> *Remember that it's motivation that gets you started, but it's habit that keeps you going.*
>
> -   *Author Unknown*

APPENDIX
RESOURCES

Patty Kreamer - www.ByeByeClutter.com

Harold Taylor - www.TaylorOnTime.com

Maria Gracia - www.getorganizednow.com

National Association of Professional
Organizers (NAPO)
www.napo.net

POWR = Professional Organizers Web Ring
www.organizerswebring.com

The DMA's Mail Preference Service (MPS)
www.the-dma.org

ORGANIZING PRODUCTS

Eldon - www.eldonoffice.com

Esselte - www.esselte.com

In2 Products - www.organizingproducts.com

Lillian Vernon ® - www.lillianvernon.com

Office Depot® - www.officedepot.com

Organize-It - www.organizeit.com

Rubbermaid® - www.rubbermaid.com

Staples® - www.staples.com

ABOUT THE AUTHOR

Patty Kreamer is the President of Kreamer Connect, Inc., a company that offers a variety of professional organizing services. Patty customizes training programs for corporations and associations, and she provides business consulting to large and small companies that want to increase the productivity and morale in the workplace.

On an individual basis, Patty helps clients discover their natural habits to successfully organize their life by using the philosophy offered in "...But I Might Need It Someday!"

Some organizations that have called upon Patty for services include: Bayer Corporation, Chatham College, The Federal Executive Board, Education Management Corporation, Alpern Rosenthal, Days Inn, and Fantastic Sams of PA.

Patty is the Founder of the Pittsburgh Professional Organizers, a qualified member of the National Speakers Association, and a member of the National Association of Professional Organizers.

Patty and her husband, George, both avid golfers, live in Pittsburgh with their cool dog, Bear.